A Gift of Understanding

Nakirega Susan

My journey to realistic Christianity

Dedication

To my mother, Proscovia Margaret Nabisubi, Mum, you saw to it that I came to know God at an early age and I am grateful for your prayers.

To all the people who donate to Bible study fellowship (BSF), from those who provide finances, to those who undertake research and to all who volunteer in different capacities. From those who type and proofread lessons to the class administrators, teaching leaders, substitute teaching leaders, discussion leaders, and children leaders, thank you for the work you do.

PROLOGUE

Many people have written books about the Christian life; however, very few have tackled the difficulty of living that life. When I decided to take my Christian life more seriously, most churches that I attended gave me the impression that the Christian life was easy and full of miracles. All I had to do was to carry all my burdens, place them on Jesus and then live a good life. With such promises in my mind, I thought my life was going to move from one victory to another. How excited I was!

In contrast to what I was told, the more I learnt about walking with God, the more I realised that I had been deceived. Difficulties became part of my life, instead of my life being easy. There are difficulties such as the guilt of sin, the burden of sin; the struggle to overcome sin, the fact that prayer is not easy, and trusting God is no joke-especially during times of trouble. Moreover, Bible study requires discipline, reflection and consistency to gain the most out of it. Most importantly, God uses pain to change us for our good. Which good is not only about giving us what we want, but also about changing our character, attitude, beliefs and behaviour to conform us to the image of Christ. These and more were some of the burdens that no one took the time to tell me.

This book is for every Christian who is experiencing hard times, as encouragement that you are on the right track. Any person whom God has changed without experiencing pain (if that is possible) to thank Him. In addition, it is for anyone who is just beginning their Christian walk, so you can know the truth, most churches rarely discuss.

This is not a new approach to Christianity, but the reality that our Lord and saviour told us about in (John 16:33). He told us to expect troubles as long as we live in this world. While this is true, He was quick to encourage us to take heart for He has overcome the world.

Looking at my life now, I am thankful to God that He has transformed me from believing everything to questioning all things, and finally to have a strong, saving faith. I have come this far because of God's love, grace, mercy and His character of long suffering. If it were not for His Grace, I would have given up and gone my own way.

Chapter 1: My memories of the war

Hymn: Though Trouble Assail Us

I was born in Uganda, in the 1980s to a single mother. I am the last born of three siblings, with an elder brother, Bogi, and sister, Jane. I believe I had a pleasant childhood because I was so doted on by my mum and because I had so many friends with whom to play. Mum loved us so much that she worked very hard to provide us with a decent life. She hired a housekeeper to care for us while she went to work. She was at work most of the time and I only saw her at night. Sunday was my favourite day of the week because Mum was around the whole day.

Playing was an important part of growing up. With the help of friends, we created toys according to the games we were going to play. My favourite was dodge ball, we would make a small ball out of banana fibres and to increase its speed, we would put a small stone inside. If you did not play well, you risked being hit hard. We also used banana fibres to make dolls. I loved my dolls and would sew dresses for them using leftover fabric I collected from the village tailor. I grew so attached to the dolls that I did not want to throw them away when they grew old. Instead, I took them to the banana plantation and told them that I was leaving them at their grandmother's place.

We incorporated cooking and hairdressing in our playtime. We stole food from our homes to practice cooking; we plaited and hot combed our hair. On one occasion, I burnt one of my playmates while hot combing her hair and my actions left her with a large wound at the back of her neck.

I hated housework. Fetching water was the only chore I enjoyed doing because we spent hours playing at the well. Yet fetching water was the only chore I was forbidden to do, as it posed a danger to my life. Given my age and height, I could easily fall into the well and drown.

Besides the well, there were other dangers all around and I did not know it. From 1980 to 1986, the country was engaged in a guerrilla war, which left many people dead and property destroyed. These were difficult times for the country. This war led to the current government gaining power. Being a pre-schooler, I only retained three memories of that war.

My first memory of the war was my sister Jane coming home from boarding school with swollen feet. Due to my family's limited finances, it was cheaper to place us in boarding school immediately after nursery school. Attending a day school meant needing money for transport every day and feeding three mouths daily. Therefore, Jane was sent to boarding school the moment she was ready for primary.

Her school was in a district called Luweero, which is 30 miles from the capital Kampala. It was in this district that the guerrilla war had started. Jane told us that, when the fighting reached their school, they had to flee on foot. They spent two days and nights travelling without food or water. During the night, they ate raw cassava from the deserted gardens. If they were lucky to find a borehole where there were no soldiers, they had a chance to quench their thirst. On reaching Kampala, they were taken to Namirembe Cathedral, and radio announcements asked parents to collect their children from the church. For people in the city, this was a shock, the war had been fought intensely for months, yet they knew nothing about it.

My second memory of the war was my brother Bogi calling me to look at soldiers who were marching towards the king's palace (Lubiri). At that time, the central government had abolished monarchies, confiscated their properties and declared the country a republic. What was once a magnificent palace had been turned into an army barracks. We were all excited to see men in uniforms carrying heavy guns and singing. However, the sound of bullets drove us quickly back home. Mum had gone to work and we were afraid to be in the house alone. We ran to the neighbour's one-room house, built of mud and wattle. We were eight young bodies squeezed under the bed. We were told to be still and quiet or else the soldiers would come and kill all of us.

The whole neighbourhood was silent. The only sounds were the barks of Beauty and Kawalya, the property owner's dogs plus the sound of bombs and bullets. With each bomb and bullet, the house shook so much that dust fell from the walls and filled the air. We must have stayed under those beds for hours, though in my young memory, it seemed like minutes. The whole experience was very scary for the adults but fun for us kids. I do not remember when Mum came back or how we returned home.

My final memory of the war was one evening when we went to Namirembe Cathedral; I do not remember why we went there. I only remember sitting in the cathedral compound with soldiers moving about, maybe seeing so many soldiers makes it memorable.

That is my side of the story, yet my mum has a different version of events. She tells me that, from 1965 (three years after Uganda's Independence) to 1986, there were around five regime changes. These changes came by bullets and not by ballots, and each regime caused difficult and unpredictable times-one minute everything was normal, and the next minute you were in trouble.

In the 1970s, mum experienced one of those days that started as normal and ended into trouble. Mum was studying for her diploma in Nakawa business school; a female police officer stopped mom and other female students at the school gate. In shifts, the students were transported on a police patrol to Nagulu prison. At the prison, they were given five strokes and had their hair cut to one inch. They were then transported to Kampala central police station, where they spent a night.

In the morning, a police officer came and started measuring the length of their skirts that is when they learnt that their crime was wearing mini-skirts. The president at that time his excellence, field marshal, conqueror of the British Empire, chancellor of Makerere University, President Idi Amin Dada had outlawed wearing short skirts. The students were sad to learn that all their skirts were of an appropriate length.

After school, mum secured a job as an accountant with Uganda hotels. The job gave us financial security; we paid our bills on time, there was food some of which mum got from work and we could afford a good education. Despite the advantages that came with the job, there were some disadvantages. It involved transfers from one hotel to another some of which were far from our home. Coupled with the country's increasing insecurity, mum was constantly worried about the safety of her children when she was away, and her security as she commuted to and from work every day.

Due to those safety worries, mum contemplated leaving her job to be with us. After weighing the advantages and disadvantages of working, financial security came up on top. Mum stayed on the job because we badly needed the money.

Another brave decision that mum made was for us to stay in our house every night. Every evening the entire village went to spend their nights at either Namirembe or Lubaga cathedrals. This was their survival tactic; for it is easier to attack people who are in solitude than those in huge numbers. For mum, it was not practical to take three toddlers with their blankets to church every night and bring them home every morning especially after a long day at work. Therefore, as the churchgoers left to seek refuge in numbers, mum sought protection from God through prayers.

Although I slept in Mum's bed until I was six, during the war it was not my permanent sleeping place. Our sleeping positions depended on the commotion outside. We slept in our beds if there were fewer movements outside. However, whenever the atmosphere was tense-such as when soldiers sat on our back veranda, discussing issues and firing bullets, we slept under the bed.

In the morning, when all the churchgoers returned, the news would spread about who had been murdered, who had been raped, whose house had been broken into and whose precious possessions had been stolen. The precious possessions usually comprised of radio cassettes and flat irons. My grandmother was once a victim of robbery and rape.

Certain events that occurred during the war are still a burden on mum's heart, and the thought of them causes her heartache. Those events include the rape of her younger sister. The day that her sister was raped had begun peacefully but then turned into an intensive afternoon. A battalion of soldiers arrived at their village in search of someone or something. All people fled to their houses and tightly locked their doors. Outside heavy footsteps and loud demands in Swahili could be heard. After an hour or so, the chaos outside was followed by silence. One by one, the people came out of their houses and news started spreading about whom the soldiers had taken.

Being concerned about her friends, Aunt Barbara (R.I.P) went to check on them. On her way, a soldier held her at gunpoint and told her to march to the nearest lodge. That soldier forced himself on her. When Barbara came back home after the supposed visit to her friends, she was quiet and withdrawn. She later confided in mum about what had happened. Mum could only look; she did not know what to say or what to do. They had no way of filing a case because both the judiciary and the police systems had broken down. Besides, Aunt Barbara did not know the name of the soldier who had raped her.

Mum also told me about the time that soldiers killed boys as they were viewed as future soldiers. Every morning, the entire village was made to assemble in one place, and boys were taken away and never seen again. It was at these times that Mum would dress my brother in a dress and make him stand in front of her, while she carried my sister on her hip. Every day, she lived in fear of losing her son.

It was during these assembling times that a neighbour's daughter was murdered. Hasifa was a beautiful and healthy girl of about seven years. On that morning, the family had woken up in preparation for the usual assembly. Hasifa was sick and had stayed in bed while her parents dressed her siblings. The soldiers then arrived at the house and started firing bullets in the air. Hasifa woke and sat up in her bed, which was a two-level bunk bed. As fate would have it, a bullet passed through the ventilator and into Hasifa's neck. She called her father, and the whole family came and surrounded her. She died hours later of a gunshot wound on the neck.

In 1978, the Tanzanian army invaded the country in an attempt to overthrow Idi Amin. Every time mum talks about the Tanzanian invasion, she also talks about a young man called John. He was a brother to one of her old classmates. John was in his twenties and travelling with his father back to their home after a visit from a family friend. John found some bullet cartridges and placed them in his bag, perhaps because he was curious about them. Consequently, the Tanzanian soldiers on a roadblock discovered John's cartridges. He was accused of being a rebel and was detained at the roadblock. Within an hour of his detention, John was shot to death in front of his protesting father. There was no investigation, no trial, and no mercy.

The war ended on 26 January 1986, when the National Resistance Army won. To this day, they remain the ruling party under the leadership of President Yoweri Kaguta Museveni. Once the war ended, I immediately joined my grandmother's nursery school, while Bogi joined Nakivubo Settlement [Primary School-a day school near our home] and Jane returned to her old school in Luweero.

The war had ended, but its effects remained with us in every area of our lives-and continue affecting us today.

15

At school, most of our games depicted our war experience-we would play war games with sticks or yam stems as guns and made the sounds of the bullets with our lips. If your playmate made the sound first, you had to fall and 'die' because the bullet had hit you. We had many toy soldiers; I do not know where they came from. We would assemble them in lines and sing war songs to them.

At one time, we visited the well and encountered a man cleaning a huge wound on his leg. The wound had deepened, exposing his bone. He told us that, during the war, he had been tortured. The wound on his leg was from soldiers burning plastic and melting the hot liquid onto his leg. Another time, we went to cut Christmas trees in the bushes near the old palace, when we found a car. Inside the car was a skeleton in the driver's seat, and we guessed the person had been a victim of the war. Sometimes we also heard stories of children who died while playing with metallic objects that exploded, they were bombs left behind after the war.

Although some semblance of peace was restored, insecurity still prevailed. Soldiers would raid houses at night, steal items and sometimes leave whole households dead. Such an incident happened near my home and, for the first time in my life, I understood what death was. In that raid, our neighbours were murdered. The couple had a son about my age, called Ssenoga, who survived yet did not understand what had happened. In the morning, I sat on our veranda and watched Senoga excitedly tell everyone who cared to listen that his mother had a hole in her breast and a nurse had put cotton wool in it. He did not know that his mother had died of gunshot wounds to the breast and he was never going to see her again. I do not know why, but I was engulfed by an emotion that I cannot explain. In my childish way, I felt for Ssenoga-I felt his loss and felt for his lack of understanding of the situation. Yet I was scared of stepping foot in their compound because I was afraid of the dead bodies. The remainder of my nursery schooling passed in peace.

Family religion

On the religious side, my family is Anglican. Every first day of the week, Mum used to send us to Namirembe Cathedral for Sunday school. This activity was compulsory unless we were sick. Our Sunday school teacher was Uncle Tom. Every Sunday, he would tell us a story from the Bible. My favourite bible story was about Zacchaeus-the short tax collector who climbed a tree to see Jesus (Luke 19:1-10). We learnt rhymes, and one of the hymns was about Zacchaeus.

Being Anglicans did not stop mum from taking us to born-again crusades. We attended crusades organised by missionaries from the United States of America and the United Kingdom. Since the country had just come out of the war, these missionaries had come to encourage Christians. The crusade I remember attending was that of Osborn.

Mum even allowed my first cousin Harriet to take us for a night prayer-the first night prayer in my life. Another time, she allowed Aunt Eve to take us to the Kampala Pentecostal Church to watch a play called Heaven's Gates and Hell's Flames. The pictures of hell were so scary that, when the pastor asked who wanted to invite Jesus into their lives, I was one of the many who stood up. This was the first among many times I was to answer the 'altar call'. In this book, I am going to mention only two-this and another one later.

When looking back on our lives, Mum sees only God's grace and mercy throughout those difficult years. She testified that we never went without food or water. There were times when she felt we were not going to make it, and then God would send an angel with food. In most cases, that angel was my grandmother, who lived two hundred meters away from us. Whenever it rained, strong winds would cause the falling of bananas in the plantation, which grandmother harvested and brought to us for food. God answered Mum's prayers for protection and provision, which she offered daily.

To this day, Mum understands the importance of food. She never throws away leftovers, unless the food has gone bad. She never allows any guest to leave her sitting room without offering them something to eat, as she imagines that the guest might be hungry. When she senses that her neighbours have no food, she sends what she can, but she also ensures she does not embarrass the recipient of her charity. She sends the food with words such as 'I know the children love to eat this, let them have it'. Mum always thanks God for food

Chapter 2; Primary school and Christianity

Hymn: Immortal, Invisible

Mum asked me to choose between two schools for my primary education, and that was Nalinya Lwantale Girls' School and Gayaza Junior School. These were both Anglican-founded schools that were products of the Church Missionary Society. Jane was in the former school, which influenced my decision to go there as well. I completed and passed the entrance interview, and started to prepare myself for this new life. The night before I was to start school, I did not sleep. I woke Mum throughout the night, asking her if it was time to get ready. That was the last time I was ever excited about going to school in seven years.

The following morning we got ready to go. Although the school was only thirty miles away, it took us two hours to get there. In the first place, we did not have a car we relied on the bus. It took the bus conductors' time to arrange our metallic suitcases and mattresses on top of the bus. We spent more time on the way while negotiating through the various security check-ups.

I found the journey to be difficult and I wished it to end in the shortest time possible. Every time I looked through the bus window, huge junks of human remains, bushes, soldiers and people met my sight. All the things I saw moved backwards as the bus moved forward. To me, we were moving in circles. By the time we reached our destination, I had a headache; I was feeling dizzy and nausea. Immediately we came out of the bus, I threw up.

I then rested under a big eucalyptus tree while mum went to the school administration block to report our arrival. It was from under this tree that I viewed my new school for the first time; it was huge with massive buildings. The buildings had bright coloured pictures of animals and maps on their walls, some of which had been drawn by the former rebels.

Mum returned from the school office to escort me to my assigned dormitory. The dormitories were named after cities of the Bible, such as Galilee, Cana, Jericho, Nazareth, Bethany and Bethlehem. Primary one dormitory Galilee was located at the end of the school perimeters bordering the school farmer and the kitchen. I do not remember how we reached my dormitory or what else happened on that day though I

21

am sure I must have waved at Mum to leave, with a big smile. I had a sister who was three classes ahead of me, and, in the dormitory, I had a friend called Grace with whom I had attended nursery school.

The first morning in my new school overwhelmed me. The matron woke us up at 5.30 am, I did not like waking up this early, yet I was going to do it for the next seven years. Our first task was to make our beds and then move outside to the veranda. On this veranda, we sang a morning hymn and thereafter said our prayers. After prayers, it was time to do dormitory work-cleaning. Sometimes we were short of water and had to fetch it from the borehole. When we finished our assigned housework, we would shower using cold water, get dressed in the blue school uniform and then march to the kitchen to eat porridge for breakfast. By 7.30 am, we were all ready to go to the assembly. This routine was for infant classes.

The upper classes woke up at 5.00 am, showered, dressed and, by 5.45 am, were already in class for morning preps. Preps ended at 7.00 am, followed by the cleaning of their classrooms. The upper classes then returned to their dormitories, completed their housework, ate their breakfast and joined the infant classes at assembly by 8.00 am.

At the assembly, we sang songs of worship, and then the matron on duty read a story from the Bible and led us in prayer. The teacher on duty told us about the activities of the day and dismissed us to our respective classes. Classes ended at 4.30 pm, after which we completed extracurricular activities, such as sports, music, dance and drama. Sometimes we visited the school farm to dig and look at the cows. Dinner was served from 5.30 to 6.30 pm, after which we sang an evening hymn, said our prayers and returned to class for evening preps until 9.00 pm for infant classes and up to 10.00 pm for upper classes.

After the evening preps, I was always hungry. I missed home and I missed mum's cooking. I missed the evening tea we used to have with mum on the veranda. I missed listening to the radio and the hot baths mum made especially for me.

When Mum came to visit every first Sunday of the month, I asked her to take me home, and she always refused. I cried at the beginning of every term and begged her not take me back to school. She never listened to my pleas.

Little did I know that having parents was a privilege. After the war, the total Ugandan population was 11 million people. The biggest portion of that population were children, some of whom had been made orphans by the war and in later years by HIV/AIDS.

A few of my classmates were orphans, and aunts and uncles were raising them. Adoption in Uganda is generally limited to family members. Adoption by non-family members occurs only for children living on the streets. Churches in the UK and US, in partnership with the Church of Uganda, did an excellent job of finding sponsors for these orphans. The orphans at my school rarely received any visitors until the end of the term. Even though my family was poor, I was in a better position than these other children were.

At the age of seven, I went through one of my most difficult years in primary school. I do not know how children without parents coped. A cold-hearted woman served as the matron for my Primary 2 dormitory, Cana. We referred to these matrons as 'Mukulu'. This mean-spirited woman used to beat us for every small mistake. On the first night in her dormitory, she instructed us to arrange our metallic suitcases beside the wall in descending order. No one stayed with her suitcase. We had to keep our edibles wrapped in plastic bags in her room, attached to the dormitory.

It was a school rule that each student must have five uniforms and no other extra clothes. These included two blue uniforms for classes, two pink uniforms for outside of class and one white uniform for the church. The matron instructed us to tie the uniforms with a string and placed them on a rope she had tied in the common room.

She selected a dorm leader whose main work was to report to her about everything we did. Every morning, the matron supervised our housework and punished us with canes if we were slow. During her reign of terror, I learnt to eat quickly, as strokes awaited the last person to reach the dormitory from the dining hall.

The most stressful times in primary two dormitory were the hours after lunch and before bedtime. After lunch, Infant students had an hour rest before resuming classes in the afternoon. We preferred to talk and play in that hour, rather than sleep. The dorm leader noted down the names of those who were talking instead of sleeping. Names appeared on that list for small talk. Sometimes my name appeared on the list. If your name was noted, you were spanked before leaving for the afternoon classes.

With time, I was relieved of this hour, as our class teacher liked me and invited me to stay at her house before I resumed classes. Therefore, every day after lunch, I lied and said that I was going to receive coaching with that teacher. She was very kind to me, though I have not seen or heard from her since Primary 2.

Although I had solved the problem of that hour, I still had to deal with the time after preps before sleep caught up with me. Like in the one-hour break after lunch, we wanted to use this time to talk and play. However, on reaching the dorm, we had to change into our nighties and go to bed, or risk punishment. I stayed awake for hours longing to return home to Mum.

On weekends, the matron would instruct us not to make noise something, which took the fun away from playing. For, we could no longer negotiate, argue, fight or celebrate a victory. We resorted to whispering in each other's ears and spend of our playtime trying to figure out what your playmate said. On seeing us whisper to each other, a woman called Teresa who used to wash our uniforms laughed and said we sounded like rats.

You needed to remain on good terms with the dorm leader because if the matron asked for the list of the people who were making noise and she did not have any, she will make up one. If the dorm leader did not like you, you were likely to appear on that list. If the dorm leader was not fast enough with the list, we all had to be punished. The matron would retrieve her guava branch rod. The first person to lie down received only one stroke, and then the strokes would increase. At such times, I hurried to be in the first 10 people so that I could receive fewer strokes.

Due to idleness, boredom and tensions caused by the matron's many don'ts, we invented games, which did not require running around. One such game involved scratching the top of the fist to remove the outer skin. The scratched area developed into a wound, which had to be taken to the dispensary for treatment. The school nurse informed the matron about what was happening. When the matron asked about it, we had no answers. What began as play escalated into something serious. Whoever had a wound on that part of the body was punished with canes-around 10 strokes each. This time I escaped because I had not joined the bandwagon. I was bothered that the dormitory leader escaped punishment after lying that her wound was caused from being scratched by a cassava branch while chasing rabbits from the matron's garden.

If anyone dared to challenge the matron or defy her orders to lie down to be beaten, she would set aside her stick and use a plastic rope. She would chase you all over the dormitory compound while beating you everywhere with the rope. From a distance, one would see an adult woman fighting a small child. By the time, her anger subsided and she let you go, you had bruises all over the body.

Yet when other matrons or teachers visited her, the matron pleasantly welcomed them and thereafter sang a song praising Jesus for His blood, which had washed all her sins away. To outsiders, this woman gave the impression that she was kind, considerate and very born again! How I hated her and longed to leave her dormitory, but there was no way to do this.

Knowing what I know now, perhaps that woman was born again, but did not have the fruit of the Spirit. She did not love any of the children under her care who were aged between six and eight years old. She was not kind, yet we needed love and understanding because our parents were far away. Maybe she was not born again after all-I could not tell.

The only time we were happy and at peace in that dormitory was when she left very early in the morning to go to town. We would play in the rest hour after lunch, and I looked forward to just lying on my bed before supper. When she returned, it meant feeling tense again. That year ended and I was more than happy to leave her dormitory.

Life in the other dormitories was good; I did not have any issues with the other dormitory leaders. I was happy except for one thing-my health declined. Between 8 and 12 years of age, I started falling sick every rainy season. The presence of stagnant water, high temperatures and the surrounding bushes provided good breeding places for mosquitos, which are the leading cause of malaria in the Tropics. I was always in and out of the school dispensary. At one time, the school nurse suggested that I sleep in the dispensary permanently because, every time she sent me to the dormitory, I fell sick again.

The frequent malaria attacks lowered my immunity, which made me vulnerable and an easy target for other diseases. I caught every epidemic the school faced. I suffered from red eyes, chickenpox and mumps. Because of the contagious nature of these diseases, anyone suffering from them was isolated in an attempt to reduce infection to others.

Thank God for modern medicine, because such diseases are not life-threatening today. I survived all of them, though they affected my life. I was very small and I met challenges in class because of absenteeism. Promotion to Primary 4 was conditional, and I eventually had to repeat a class, which made me sad. On a positive note, the older I grew, the more my immunity improved. By the time I left primary school, the number of times I fell sick had decreased to once a year.

As I was battling my illnesses and failures, a new killer disease called HIV/AIDS struck the country. The disease spread fast in the late 1980s and early 1990s and affected most families. Millions of people died slowly and in great pain, without any hope of recovery because there was no cure. The psychological pain experienced by both the sick person and the caretaker was immense. Adults tried as much as they could to shield children from what was happening, yet somehow the children still came to know.

Children who lived with the knowledge that one or both of their parents had HIV/AIDS lived in constant fear. They experienced the fear of not knowing when their parent was going to die and what would happen to them if their parent died. That fear intensified when a child at my school received a visitor on a day that was not a visitation Sunday. That meant only one thing-that either their mum or dad had passed on. This child was released to bury her loved one and thereafter returned to resume her studies.

When these children returned to school, I imagined the pain they were experiencing. I wanted to help them but did not know how to approach a person experiencing psychological pain. I was afraid to ask them how they felt, or if they wanted to talk about their loss. In the end, I avoided talking about death and pretended that nothing had happened. I limited my conversations to topics that were school-related and not home related.

Stories of children whose parents had died were heart breaking. Siblings were separated after burial, as circumstances did not permit those children to mourn together. This occurred when the deceased parents had more than two children and had left little or no resources to care for those children. The practical approach was for family members to divide those children into different homes to enable a suitable upbringing. Some children were fortunate enough to mourn and grow up together. Moreover, parents were not the only ones affected by HIV/AIDS-many children also lost younger siblings who had contracted HIV/AIDS from their mothers in the process of mother-to-child transmission.

With the rampage of the AIDS epidemics, the school administration made sure that we understood HIV/AIDS so that we did not become victims. Our teachers created school plays, poems and songs about HIV/AIDS and sexual education was necessary in upper classes. The school went further and engaged people from The AIDS Support Organization (TASO) to offer us a first-hand experience of what it meant to live with HIV/AIDS. The young men and women from TASO told us how they had contracted HIV/AIDS, how painful the disease was, and how they managed the signs and symptoms of HIV/AIDS. We were encouraged not to stigmatise people with HIV/AIDS, as they needed much love and care. Most of all, we were taught that not everyone with HIV/AIDS had contracted it through sin.

We were then encouraged to wait for marriage before indulging in any sexual activity and to respond to any sexual advances with the words 'no I am sorry'.

I received the best primary education that Uganda had to offer and I am grateful for all my experiences. I am the person I am today because of those experiences. Would I change anything? Yes, knowing what I know now, the HIV/AIDS information was good; but as a Christian school, I think they should have done better. I wish they had added that battle to preserve one 'self for marriage is not easy, it requires a close walk with God and waiting. Besides, waiting is not easy.

Religion at school

From a spiritual perspective, the school leaders tried to show us the right way to live for God by example and through teaching us the Bible. All school staff-teachers, matrons and security guards-were either single or married. School staff were supposed to be our role models for life. As students, we addressed all school staff with their proper titles of Mr, Mrs or miss respectively. Every female teacher who became pregnant outside wedlock was expelled from the school.

Truthfully, I never understood the Bible stories that were taught to us every day at assembly. This was because I applied them to my life literally. For example, the story of Jesus telling his disciples that he would make them fishers of men. I thought it meant they were to catch fish and sell them at the market. In the stories of God appearing to Abraham, I imagined Abraham was walking and a figure appeared in the clouds before him. I also started asking God to appear to me, and every time I asked, I would look up at the skies to see if a figure would appear.

All the Bible stories were beautiful and the most I learnt from them was what happens when I sin and to ask God for what I wanted. Until the study of the Ten Commandments, I did not understand sin. Moreover, when I understood sin, the sins that came to my realisation were stealing and lying. I used to love licking sugar and, in most cases, I stole it from the kitchen cabinet. I lied about many things-from where I lived to whom I played with during recess. Every time I committed those sins, I remembered the reverend's words-that thieves and liars will not enter heaven.

The love of sugar and playing made me long to grow fast and live an independent life. I always thought that, when I grow up, I would find a job, so I could buy and lick all the sugar I want. I would not have rules and regulations to follow, and I could then stop lying about who was my friend and who was not. Back then, I thought that sin was limited to actions, and not to the thoughts and motives of the heart.

When I was eight years, I decided to put the theory of God to the test. I started praying that, if God was there, let him make my mum send more snacks. I prayed every day and before long, Mum sent me a parcel through the school office full of things to eat. How I wish I had kept that prayer for later years when I faced serious life difficulties.

As a Christian school, attending church was compulsory for all students, except the Muslims. Protestants attended a nearby church, while Catholics went to the bordering secondary school, and the Muslim students stayed to enjoy playing and sleeping in the dormitory. Muslim students performed their prayers every Friday.

During Lent, there were services every evening until Easter. From the age of 11, we were encouraged to study confirmation, and our parents had to bring our baptism certificate. I enrolled for confirmation at age 11, then dropped out and re-joined at age 12. The second time I was serious and went through the classes up to the end, but there was a problem-Mum had not sent my baptism certificate.

On the Sunday before the confirmation ceremony, there was a baptism, so I decided to stop waiting for the certificate and instead be baptised again. It went well and the Bishop came the following Sunday to confirm us. The parents who could afford to do so came early in the morning with white dresses for their children. I had an idea of Mum's difficult financial status, so I prayed for a miracle. By 9.30 am, there was no sight of Mum, so I dressed in my white Sunday uniform and entered the church, with a fake smile.

After the service, I found Mum waiting for me outside with my now useless baptism certificate. She informed me that she had not received my letter and thought that confirmation was scheduled for the following month. Besides, she did not have money for the white dress.

Again, at the age of 12, I received Jesus Christ as my Lord and saviour. This occurred during a Sunday service at school led by a guest preacher. He was a white man from either the UK or US. Apart from his opening statement, I do not remember any other thing he said because I was absent-minded throughout his sermon. I was alerted when he asked if there was a person who wanted to be a friend of Jesus. Since no one went forward, I felt sorry for him. He had travelled a long distance and invested a lot of money in what he was doing, yet no one stood to show that they had understood his sermon.

I went forward to encourage him that he was a good preacher and to let him know that it was not a waste of money and time. On reaching the altar, one more person joined me. This guest preacher took us through the sinner's prayer. He asked us what we wanted, and I asked for wisdom-not because I needed it, but because we had been taught that King Solomon asked God for wisdom and that it pleased Him. Our guest encouraged me to read the Bible daily and, in that way, I would have all the wisdom in the world.

Although I had accepted Christ before, this was the first person to take me through the sinner's prayer and note my name down. I believe that this preacher and my mum continued praying for me by name, which is why I have included him in my testimony. Today I might be a Christian because of his prayers.

I also felt the hand of God on me during a dormitory situation. When we were in infant classes, there was a person who used to wash out clothes for us, and then we began washing our clothes at the age of 10. It took me longer than other students to learn how to wash clothes and polish my shoes. I was always dirty and shabby. I was too lazy to organise my possessions and my trunk was a mess. For that reason, one Saturday, my trunk was on my mind, so, while my classmates went to collect water at the borehole, I stayed behind and organised it. That same day, the matron visited me to inspect my trunk and found all my clothes folded, I was saved from a spanking. I later learnt that one of my neighbours had told the matron about the state of my trunk, and that is why she came to inspect the situation. God must have put the thought of organising my trunk into my mind.

Chapter 3; Lured by Islam

Hymn: He Leadeth Me

After primary school and more so after confirmation, the home rule that had made attending Sunday services compulsory stopped. Mum no longer forced me to attend church; she gave me the freedom to make my own decisions. She felt that she had done her duty of showing me the way and that the rest was up to me- either to go in the direction of the church or find something else. In later years, she informed me that she had prayed for me every day to make the right decision.

As a teenager, I rebelled against all the values taught to me when I was a child. I made friends with people who were much older than I was, and they influenced my decisions both positively and negatively. Consequently, those friends introduced me to clubs and alcohol. In spite of what people say about alcohol it did not appeal to me, I found it to be bitter and with a disgusting.Smell.

It was time to move from primary to secondary school. With my newfound freedom, I decided against going to traditional schools. I chose a new Muslim girls' private school around town. My new school was the exact opposite of my primary school. It was near home, we were allowed to grow our hair as long as it remained natural, and attending church was optional. There were no morning preps, and this made me happy because I could now enjoy some morning sleep!

For the next six years, I did not think of changing schools; that was how much I loved my new school-or, rather, that was how much I resented my former school. I made many friends and, up to today, many of my friends are Muslims. There were new subjects to study at this level, including Islamic religious education and Arabic. I loved the former because it had stories similar to those in the Bible, but I disliked the Arabic language because I could not relate to it in any way.

Tutored in Islam

The first lesson in Islam was the definition of the religion, which involves total submission to the will of Allah and obedience to His laws. There were two papers of Islam to study: Paper 1 was the history of Islam and Paper 2 was about the holy Quran.

As in Christianity, the father of all believers in Islam is Ibrahim. Muslims believe that Ibrahim lived in Mecca with his wife, Sarah, who was infertile. After years of trying to conceive without success, Sarah suggested to her husband to marry her maid, Hajara, who was from Egypt. Hajara gave Ibrahim a son called Ismail. Contrarily, Sarah was jealous of Hajara and her baby, so she ordered Ibrahim to chase them away.

Ibrahim took Hajara and Ismail and left them in the desert with a skin of water and some dates. When they finished the water, Hajara could not bear to watch the baby as he died of dehydration, so she left him and began to run from Salaf hill to another hill called Marwa in search of water. After running back and forth, she heard a voice coming from the valley between the hills. When she looked there, she saw an angel digging a well with his heel. This became Hajara's Well and it acquired the name Zam Zam.

A similar story exists in the Bible, but the difference lies in the individual who God selected to carry on the blessing. While the Bible insists that God blessed Isaac, the Quran says that Allah selected Ismail as the person through whom the world would be blessed. Allah commanded Ibrahim to sacrifice Ismail, who he substituted for a lamb. That day became important for Ibrahim and his followers. Allah also commanded Ibrahim to build the Kaaba on the site, which he achieved with the help of Ismail. Ibrahim and Ismail then began to pray to Allah to send a prophet to the people of Mecca, as well as a book. In answer to that prayer, Allah sent the Prophet Mohammad and the holy Quran.

Islam Paper 2 began with the coming of the Prophet Mohammad and the holy Quran. The Prophet Mohammad was born in 570 AD in the city of Mecca in the Quraysh clan. His parents died when he was young, so his uncle Abu Talib took him in. Being uneducated, Mohammad participated in the silver and hides trade over long distances to earn a living. He worked for an older wealthy woman called Khadijah, who later became his first wife. Mohammad was a humble boy and his trustworthiness made him popular throughout Mecca.

One day, Mohammad was sleeping in a cave during the holy month of Ramadan, when the angel Gabriel visited him. Gabriel commanded Mohammad to read what he had put before him, but Mohammad could not read because he was uneducated. Gabriel then pressed

Mohammad's body hard repeating the same command to read. On Gabriel's persistence, Mohammad managed to read what was before him, which was the first portion of the Quran. Mohammad returned home and told his wife Khadijah what had happened, she told him not to be afraid because he was a prophet. From that time on, Mohammad faced opposition and hatred, and Khadijah became his source of comfort and encouragement.

Islam began with that revelation, and the religion is built on five pillars. The most important of these pillars is to bear witness that there is no god except Allah and that Mohammad (PBUH) was his messenger. I learnt that, whenever a Muslim mentions the name 'Mohammad', she or he must include the phrase 'peace be upon him'. The Muslim god, Allah, is not begotten, so he cannot beget anyone. He does not produce and thus does not have any children. He does not look like anything in the universe. He has 99 names, which are written at the start of the Quran. The day he is most angry is Christmas because people in the universe have associated Him with a mere human-that he has a son. Every Christmas, Allah feels like commanding all the mountains, hills and water bodies to cover up the earth and kill all people, except for the few who worship him. However, because of his great love and mercy for human beings, he waits to give all people a chance to turn to him.

Prayer is another pillar on which Islam stands. Every Muslim must pray five times a day. The first prayer must be performed before sunrise and is called Subuhi; if it is performed after sunrise, it is nullified. The second prayer is performed between the hours of noon and 4.00 pm and is called Zuhuli. Aswiri is performed between 4.00 pm and 6.00 pm, while Maghrib is performed between 7.00 pm and 8.00 pm. The final prayer, Isha, is performed between 8.00 pm and dawn. Prayers can be performed alone, but it is more rewarding to perform them in a congregation. The first person in the mosque for prayers receives rewards equivalent to five camels, while the last person receives a reward equivalent to an egg.

Before prayers, one must have the intention to pray and then proceed to perform ablution. During ablution, one must pour water in the hair to reach the scalp, and then wash the face and rinse the mouth three times. One then washes the arms from the fingers to the elbow three times and then washes the feet. If one has engaged in sexual activities or masturbation, had a wet dream, had a menstrual period or undergone childbirth, one must wash the whole body from head to toe with clean water in a ritual called gusulu before engaging in any kind of prayers. Prayers must be performed while facing the holy Qabaa in Mecca or the prayers are nullified. There is a separation of men and women during congregational prayers. A man must cover everything between the navel and the knees, while a woman must cover all her body, except for her palms and face, if her prayers are to reach Allah.

Islam demands that all adult Muslims fast during the holy month of Ramadan. The only people exempt from fasting are children under 12 years of age, the sick, the elderly, pregnant women, nursing mothers and women who are experiencing their menstrual cycle. Fasting begins from sunrise to sunset, and people must go through the day without water or food. All people fasting must behave in a manner pleasing to Allah, and he rewards all those who fast and those who provide food to break the fast in the evening. The last 10 days of Ramadan are important because one of them might be Leila-tul-kadam (the 'night of power'). This 'night of power' is the day on which the Prophet Mohammad received the first portion of the Quran. If that day finds you in prayer, Allah grants you your entire request.

Every Muslim must pay zakat depending on his wealth. Zakat translated as alms, is to help a Muslim understand that they do not own wealth and that everything belongs to Allah. In other words, Muslims must eliminate excessive agreed, which is lured to them by their desires. They must, therefore, discipline themselves by giving and supporting the poor out of the wealth blessed to them by Allah. Zakat is paid annually.

Visiting the holy Qabaa in Mecca is the last pillar of Islam. Allah demands that every able-bodied Muslim with sufficient resources must visit the holy Qabaa in Mecca-a ritual called hajji. Hajji is completed during the month of dhulu hajj. Muslims run around the Qabaa-a building that covers one mile-seven times. Afterwards, pilgrims run from the hill Salaf to the hill Marwa, and then stone Satan. If a pilgrim dies while performing hajji, his soul goes straight to heaven. Pilgrims acquire the title of 'hajji' for men and 'hajjat' for women and return home sinless-they return to their homes like new-born babies. If you are weak but have money, you can pay someone to perform hajji on your behalf.

Some facets of Islam, the Prophet Mohammad and the Quran left me convinced that Islam was a true religion from God. For example, the Islamic calendar, which began when the Prophet Mohammad migrated from Mecca to Medina (hijra), aligns perfectly with the lunar system. Surely, that was the work of God, I thought to myself. Moreover, the prophet, an illiterate person, managed to receive the whole Quran as we have it today. Unlike the Bible, the Quran is not arranged in chronological order because it was revealed according to the needs of the people. If the people's need was prayer, Allah would send an angel to the prophet telling him how and when Muslims should pray.

When reading the Quran, one notices that the chapters revealed in Mecca differ from those revealed in Medina because the needs of the people were different. Islam first spread in Mecca; however, because people were not ready to listen, the chapters revealed in that area were short, precise and poetic-fit for people who were on the move and not ready to listen. On the other hand, the chapters revealed in Medina were long, elaborative and included laws governing a state to suit people who were settled, ready to listen and ready to build an Islamic state.

I was left thinking that Islam was one of the many religions that can lead you to the one true God. My primary school mathematics teacher led me to develop the idea that there were many routes to heaven. Each time he gave us an equation to solve, he also gave us different alternatives on how to reach the answer, with the statement 'there are so many routes to Heaven'. However, although I found Islam amazing, I never thought about converting to the religion until I visited the school mosque. Dalasa (sermons) were organised by the school administration and were compulsory for Muslim students. Non-Muslim students were invited to attend if they wished. I responded positively to an invitation out of curiosity.

A sheikh gave the sermon, which almost converted me to Islam. The sermon discussed what happens when we die and what will happen on the last day of judgement. The sheikh taught that, before we die, each one of us is shown where we are going after death- heaven or hell. If someone has lived a righteous life in the way that the Quran teaches, she or he is shown hell first and then heaven. The reverse is true for people who have been non-believers. This explains why some people die with smiles on their faces, while others fight in the face of death because they have seen where they are going.

In the grave, the body regains consciousness and starts experiencing underground punishment. The first punishment is for all people, whether they are Muslims or non-Muslims. The ribs of the dead person are squeezed hard until they bypass each other. According to Islam, the first day in the grave is the hardest. Two grave angels, Munkar and Nakir, come to examine you. These angels are very dark, almost purplish, and scary. They ask you three questions: Who is your God? What is your religion? What do you believe about the Prophet Mohammad? For each question that you fail, an axe from a high mountain hits your head, and your body moves 70 yards underground. The body then undergoes other punishments. What I understood on that day was that the body would not rest until the resurrection.

On the last day of judgement, the sun and moon will not provide light-it will be total darkness. However, the believers will have light to guide them, as the body parts that they bathed every day before prayers will be shining. Each person will appear before Allah to give an account of his or her life, and it is from these accounts that some people will go to hell, while others will go to heaven. Islam believes that an individual enters heaven based on both faith and actions.

On the day of judgement, the prophet's favourite uncle will experience the least of all punishments-he will wear shoes that are blazing with fire, boiling his brain. If that is going to be the least punishment, I wondered what would happen to me. Much as some punishments were hard, some had a touch of humour, such as the genital organs of every person you slept with outside of marriage appearing on your face.

The sheika told us that we could experience the blazing fire of hell here on earth by putting the index fingers in our ears and listen. The sound that you hear is the blazing fire in hell.

These sermons left me terrified. I was afraid of both death and the punishments that are to follow. I started thinking of converting to Islam because of the fear of punishment. Note that my thoughts about conversion to Islam were not only about fear but also included positive elements that stayed in my mind. I was encouraged by my friends' words and behaviour. They told me in a gentle way that Christianity was not going to lead me to heaven. If I intended to reach heaven, I should consider Islam. These friends had formed strong bonds, despite their different backgrounds, because of their strong faith. They were always quick to forgive each other by saying 'salaam aleiku' (peace be upon you), whenever they disagreed. Muslims girls behaved well and did not lie or steal. In everything they did, their first motive was to please Allah, their God.

Unlike men, who have to endure circumcision upon conversion to Islam, for a woman, it is very simple. All I had to do was take a ritual bath; touch the Quran with my right hand and pledge allegiance to the one true God, Allah, and Mohammad is his prophet and messenger. After saying those words, I would have become a Muslim woman.

My friends highlighted the many rewards I would receive if I became a Muslim. The first reward was to be forgiven all my sins to the status of a new-born baby. If I were to die after my conversion, I would go straight to heaven.

I had some questions for my friends, and they answered these questions while quoting the Quran. One of my main concerns was the issue of marrying many wives. They told me that the true Islamic faith indirectly forbids adultery. How? I asked. They told me that the conditions that are set for a man to have a second wife are almost impossible to follow. These conditions include having the resources to look after two wives and loving both wives equally. I think it is impossible to love two men or in this case two different women equally. Moreover, before a man takes a second wife, he must seek permission from the first wife. My friends were of the view that, if a man loves Allah, he will marry only one wife.

Marriage to a Muslim brings more rewards, especially for the woman. Islam allows a woman to ask for a dowry from her husband on their wedding day. A Muslim woman must be paid by her husband for breastfeeding their children. A woman who dies in child labour goes straight to heaven because she died while bringing a new life on earth. The Muslim faith is the only religion that has made all people equal on earth. How so? I asked. I was told that when death occurs, for Muslims there is no difference in burial arrangements between the poor and rich. Men are buried in three sheets while women are buried in five sheets regardless of their financial status.

My Muslim friends loved me and did not want me to go to hell, so they took the time to answer my questions patiently and encouraged me to accept Islam smoothly. Yet, somehow, I could not bring myself to publically say the words that there is no god but Allah and Mohammad his prophet and messenger. However, whenever I thought my life was in danger, I said those words with the hope of entering paradise if I were to die that day.

From Islam to Christian religious education

On joining the Advanced Level of education (A-level), I decided to drop Islam and try Christian religious education. The syllabus started by debating the authorship of the first five books of the Bible and later explored the differences between Genesis Chapters 1 and 2. That syllabus did not support a logical case for Christianity-I had never known that the first two chapters of Genesis conflicted with each other.

The New Testament was even more boring. It involved Paul defending his apostleship, Paul quarrelling with other apostles or writing angry letters to people who were moving away from his teachings. I wished to drop the subject but had already started, so there was no chance of quitting. I endured until the end of the study and attained a passing grade.

On my spiritual path, I was now a Christian by name only. For six years, I think I attended church twice. Much as the school had been founded on the Islamic faith, Christians had the freedom to worship. Christian students who wished to do so, organise a service every Sunday. The people interested cleaned one classroom as the place of worship and then decided who was to preach and how to use the offertory money.

I owned a small Gideon New Testament Bible, which included the Book of Psalms and Book of Proverbs. Every now and then, I read a psalm, depending on what I was going through. I used fasting as a means of getting what I wanted from God. Sometimes it worked, but, on other occasions, it failed.

The future fascinated me; I wanted to know what would happen to me and, if possible, I intended to control it. I stole a book from my mum, which had belonged to her father. It was an old book called *Napoleon's Book of Fate*. I used it to try to predict the future, even though some of its pages had faded and others had fallen out. I went to the largest bookshop in town to buy a new one but was disappointed to learn that it was out of print. However, I would not leave the bookshop empty-handed instead; I bought a book about palm reading. I occupied some of my school time by studying my palm to glimpse my unknown future. I also started reading the palms of my friends. I took this obsession about the future further by reading newspaper horoscopes

Nevertheless, my mum continued to pray for me.

Chapter 4; A Surprising call

Hymn: Be Thou My Vision

In my later teens, I realised that all my life I had been hearing about God, yet I did not know who He was. I found myself wanting to know Him experientially. I had developed a vacuum in my heart, which I could not ignore. This feeling led me to move from one church to another with the hope of seeing God.

A friend who believed that her church had been empowered by the Holy Spirit recommended the first pastor I visited. Tuesday was the only day of the week when that pastor met new members for a one-on-one counselling. Come Tuesday, my friend and I met at the taxi stage, from where we proceeded to a place that I thought was going to change my life. With little traffic, we arrived a few minutes after 7.00 am.

The first thing I noticed was the absence of a church; rather, there was a house with a cemented compound. In the middle of the compound was a small, raised circle, like a small roundabout, and on the circle was written the words 'Jesus is the answer'. With Jesus being the answer, I wondered what could be the question.

An elderly man opened the garage door, where we sat on a bench. I moved around the house and noticed that all the rooms were open except for the one room at the end of the corridor. Later I learnt it was the counselling room. As we waited for the pastor, other people joined us.

After we had waited for hours, the pastor finally arrived some minutes after 10.00 am driving a black SUV. He was light-skinned with pink lips, slightly obese and slightly lame in one leg. One by one, we entered the counselling room. Some people took a long time in that room, while others took only a few minutes.

When my turn came, I was admitted into a tidy and carpeted room. One wall was adorned with a framed picture of Jerusalem. Below the picture was a single sofa occupying the room. The pastor sat on the sofa, while I knelt before him. He greeted me nicely and asked what my problem was. I did not tell him about the need in my heart to know God because I did not know how to express my need in words. I instead told him that I wanted to be admitted to one of the top universities in the country. We prayed together about my need, though I did not experience God's power, which he had promised would come strongly upon me in prayer.

After that short prayer, the pastor told me about an upcoming powerful service, he asked me to attend the service with my mom. I assured him that I would be there, though my mum would not accept because she did not like me attending his counselling sessions. Mum was of the view that Jesus met people in public and not in private rooms, though, as usual, she did not stop me from attending. When the date for the big day service arrived, I left home early, eager to hear God's powerful word and to see many miracles, signs and wonders. I secretly prayed to experience God's miracle-working power first hand. With time, I leant that the pastor organised one service in a month called the big day service.

I arrived at around 9.30 am for my first big day service and almost missed a seat because of the large number of people. We started with praise and worship, which continued for a long time, but the pastor was nowhere in the picture. He only arrived after 11.00 am with his wife, a beautiful light-skinned woman. They sat at the platform and behind them hung a yellow banner with words from Psalms 77:14 in black ink, reading 'you are the God who performs miracles; you display your power among the People'. The pastor opened the service with a short prayer and thereafter called people to give testimonies to glorify the name of the lord and encourage others in the faith.

The testimonies included the usual everyday needs of individuals, such as God's provision of jobs after many years of trying; provision of salvation to family members and friends; protection against accidents and theft; and God's love, mercy and peace following His people. Then they moved to the things that I had read in the bible but had never experienced.

It was at this church that I met couples looking for babies. The number of people in search of miracle babies overwhelmed me; I had always thought that after marriage, the next thing is a baby. Yet these people testified that they had failed to conceive for years. While others said that they only managed to conceive after the pastor had prayed for them.

Furthermore, were the people who had enough faith to seek supernatural healing. A woman testified that she had been suffering from mental illness, but because of the pastor's prayers, she had been healed. This was strange because, from a young age, I was always encouraged to go to the hospital whenever I fell sick. After the decision was made that I needed to see a doctor, we would then pray to God to give the doctor wisdom to determine the correct diagnosis and right prescription.

As I was still digesting the supernatural healing, I heard from a man who had been delivered from a 'spiritual wife'. The young man said that, before he had joined the pastor's fellowship, a woman used to visit him in the night and they were intimate. He had seen this woman numerous times, yet could not describe her because she only visited when the lights were off. She would come in the middle of the night and leave before dawn. The existence of this spiritual wife had made marriage for this young man impossible. However, through prayer and fasting, the spiritual wife was chased in favour of a human wife.

The testimony of a spiritual spouse left me with more questions and fewer answers. Who are these 'spiritual husbands and wives'? How do they operate? How many people have experienced a spiritual spouse? Does the Bible talk about spiritual spouses? Maybe the young man was just fantasizing in his sleep.

Some people had demons. During the powerful prayer session, the pastor would call out the people with demons and ask the demons who had sent them and why. Afterwards, he would command the demons to leave the individuals. The people possessed with demons would shout, jump and roll on the ground. I was impressed that the pastor could see and talk with the demons.

There was a testimony, which made me jealous. It was a testimony from a man who told us about how he had received a vision. He told us how he had fasted and sought the face of God during the Easter holidays. Come Easter Sunday, he had a vision in which Jesus visited him. Jesus told him that, just as He had resurrected on that Sunday, he was going to resurrect all this man's dreams.

I was jealous because that was my desire, to see Jesus. Back then, I would have done anything to have the same vision.

After the jealous, I moved on to questioning God's character of omnipresence. This happened after the assistant pastor told us how God had strengthened and comforted him after he had lost his brother. The senior pastor had intervened by telling him how his relatives had used evil powers to finish off his brother. Moreover, that God had chased away those evil powers but the relatives had persisted. The last time they had sent the evil powers, God had left the place and that is why his brother had died.

The senior pastor's words got me thinking, doesn't God supposed to be everywhere. If God did not want the brother to die, for sure He is more powerful than all the evil forces in the world. I decided that the God of that pastor was not worth following if He could not deal with those evil powers effectively and if He could not be in two places at the same time.

I then moved on to the next fellowship. This fellowship was unique because the senior pastor was a woman. Her luxurious life astonished me. She had a fancy car with a chauffeur; she dressed in expensive clothes and high heels. I loved her shoes. Some members of her church happily volunteered to carry her bible and handbag to and from the pulpit.

If I thought the testimonies from the first fellowship I visited strange, the testimonies in this church were stranger. The first testimony that left me scratching my head came from a woman who testified that she been healed of AIDS. That woman narrated how her husband had died of AIDS and how she panicked thinking that she too was going to die of the disease. She had come to church and with the support of the pastor; they had prayed and believed for healing. When she went for a blood test, she was negative, thus giving the glory to God.

After that testimony, the pastor told us that AIDS and all other chronical diseases are demons, which can be managed by prayer, and fasting. She read a few lines from the bible, which I do not remember and thereafter asked if someone was looking for healing. When the majority answered positively, the pastor told us that we needed to give if God was to move faster in our lives. She selected one person from the congregation and told him that she had seen rain falling on him and therefore it was his day for God to bless him.

She turned to the congregation and asked us to present the blessed man with a car. No person moved, she challenged anyone with AIDS and wanted to heal to give out his/her car away. Again, there was no response. The pastor went on and on about giving away a car in exchange for healing and we were all quite. Towards the end, someone gave away his car keys to the blessed person. At last, the pastor gave the closing prayer and we were dismissed.

For many days to come, I could not bring myself to forget about the AIDS healing testimony. To begin with, why didn't that woman carry out a blood test to confirm that she was HIV positive before praying? Was there someone in the church who knew about her husband to confirm her story? Maybe it was one of the rare cases of discordant couples. Why didn't other people dying of AIDS come and experience this supernatural healing as well? The debate in my mind was endless.

I believe that with God, all things are possible; but I could not believe that without medical intervention, AIDS could be healed

I continued visiting the fellowship even though I felt my need of knowing God was not being met. One afternoon I felt the emptiness inside my heart was growing bigger and bigger. I decided to go for the Sunday evening service thinking that maybe something will be said to lift my moods. The assistance pastor was leading that service. In his opening statement, he said that when it comes to money, we should not give up. That we should pray, fast and give to God until He makes us rich.

On hearing those words, I became restless in both mind and body. I could no longer hear what he was saying, as my mind wandered off to other things. My body could not sit still. After ten or fifteen minutes of this restlessness, I moved out of the church well knowing that I will never return.

I had exchanged one church for another in the search for God, and I had not found Him. I instead found both churches preaching wealth, health and a good life. I had seen demons chased from people, yet no demon came out of me. I had met people who had been healed supernaturally yet I had not experienced any supernatural healing. People had seen Jesus yet I had not seen him anywhere. Pastors called people to the pulpit to prophecise to them about their future yet I was never singled out. Others had experienced answered prayers in all forms yet my prayer of seeing God was not answered. It became clear to me that if I had any hopes of seeing God, I should look elsewhere.

Stumbled by rudeness

Most people I told about my church experience were of the view that I lacked faith and that was the reason I never experienced God's miracle-working power. Others said that I reasoned a lot while others were of the view that I was looking at people and pastors instead of looking at God. It was during those times that I wondered if there was something wrong with me and not the church.

However, I reminded myself that by going to church every Sunday was faith enough. About reasoning, I sincerely believe that we have been called to be reasoning and not just believing Christians. Besides, much as it is true that we must look up to God, it is also true that we need human guidance. If I do not look up to my pastor for spiritual guidance, then whom should I look up to.

Fortunately, one of my friends was also having issues with the modern church. Cissy (R.I.P) had attended different churches from the ones I had attended but she too was giving up.

Her reasons for giving up were very different from mine; they had to do with how some pastors behaved. She narrated to me how a pastor in one of the churches she had attended had asked all those who did not have plots of land to stand up. Having nothing written to her name, Cissy too stood up. The pastor then asked them where their faith was. He wondered how they could call themselves born again, and yet have no land on which to build houses. He made it seem as though their lack of plots was due to their little faith in God. The pastor proceeded to brag about his wealth that included a bungalow with his private pool in his compound. A car that did not require him to bend as he entered the driver's seat. He called those material things rewards of faith.

Cissy had ignored the pastor's bragging but what she could not ignore was how he treated his junior pastor. He talked down at him as if he was a two-year-old. He used demeaning words when asking him to do small things like giving a closing prayer. Moreover, that treatment was continuous, almost every Sunday. That disrespect of his juniors coupled with self-entitlement forced her to look for another church.

Cissy then visited many churches but it was hard to find one, which could cater to her needs. In the end, she concluded that there was no perfect church and therefore settled for the one which was near her home.

In her new church, Cissy overlooked all the church dysfunction and concentrated on learning the good that was being taught about God and Jesus. That was until she invited her friend Carol (R.I.P) for a healing service. Since Carol needed the healing badly, they went early to occupy the front seats. When the pastor noticed them, he sent an usher to ask Carol to sit in the back pews because she was not 'looking good'. Carol infected with HIV had all the visible signs of the disease. She was humble enough to accept that request and moved to the back pews.

When it was time to pray for the sick, carol quickly moved forward. The pastor rudely asked who had brought her to the front. He reluctantly laid his hands on her and commanded all her illness to leave her in Jesus' name. The pastor took less time when praying for Carol compared to other people who looked healthier. Carol passed away soon afterwards, and Cissy could never forget that Sunday service. We all wondered why the pastor was not kind to a sick person. If we who were not role models for a huge number of people managed to be kind, why not a person who was looked at by many for guidance?

Cissy and I further discussed other issues happening in the church, which we felt were not right. The most common wrong that modern churches are doing is preaching God's word selectively. Church leaders are shy when it comes to rebuking, correcting, disciplining and training in righteousness. They centre their sermons on giving back to God, which amounts to exploitation and false promises.

As long as you are a good giver, the church will never talk about the wrongs that you are doing, not even in privacy. They will praise and cover up all your indiscretions with sweet words. Like the way, the church in Uganda is promoting dictatorship by portraying a president who has been in power for more than three decades as the best thing that has ever happened to the country. This presentation is not only limited to the local scene but it is extended on the international platform. American Christian television TBN portrayed the Ugandan president as a Moses who led his people from the wilderness of Idi Amin to the Promised Land where people have freedom of worship. It is rumoured and widely believed that the president sends these church leaders money for those campaigns.

It is a shame that these church leaders do not care what the common people experience living in a country with no healthcare, no jobs and no hope, yet burdened with heavy taxes. Sometimes I think that these leaders are loyal to the president because he has created an atmosphere in which poor people must go to church to find hope.

In most cases, this hope comes in the form of false promises. Some cold church leaders who claim to hear from God directly will tell the hopeless exactly what they long to hear. They tell sick people especially those suffering from AIDS and cancer to put aside their medication to leave room for Jesus to heal them. Those without jobs that Jesus is soon opening a door for them. Whatever the problem, pastors will tell you to plant a seed and leave the rest to Jesus.

With those promises, an individual can be kept in a vicious cycle of hope, which will make or break him. The false promises make individuals by motivating them to look deeper in what they are following. Such people usually move away from such churches and instead find a true saving faith. On the other hand, some people are broken to the extent of being hostile to God.

After those observations, Cissy decided to continue to seek until she could find a place where she could feel comfortable. I cannot tell whether she found that place because, in the last days of her life, we did not talk much. I had gone away for further studies as she continued to struggle in Uganda.

On my side, I was tired of moving from one church to another, so I then made television my church. I used to watch many Christian programmes;-I enjoyed some and disapproved of others. After all this moving around, there was something, which had changed inside me. I did not believe everything I heard; —I had become a critical person. I could develop a feeling of peace every time I watched a program with which I felt comfortable with, and the reverse was true in case I was watching a program of which I disapproved. Sometimes I could get restless until I switched off the television. In addition, another reality hit me—the gospel of financial prosperity was not limited to poor Africans, but also to rich countries in America and Europe.

It was during this period that I discovered a teaching that was going to become a stumbling block for most of my Christian walk. It happened one morning when I was watching some pastor on television who said ''wherever there is a Jewish person, there is God. That statement got me thinking, what the pastor meant. Did he mean that, if God's presence is shared in percentages, where there is a Jewish person, God is there eighty percent while the rest of the world struggled for his attention with the 20%? Is it true that the Lord God practices favouritism? What did the pastor really mean? I had no answers and just decided to ignore such teachings and. I thought the Jewish issue would go away, but it instead came back in a different style.

Another preacher testified that God had blessed his ministry beyond his dreams because of his support for Israel. He further instructed his followers who wanted to be blessed to give money in support of Israel and to always pray for Israel. Israel again! I thought to myself. So, does he mean that, if I want to increase my chances of God's blessing, I should give and pray for Israel, and not my immediate neighbours? I resented this teaching; I could not believe that a fair and loving

God had favoured and less-favoured believers. I just could not believe it.

Meanwhile, I gained new ideas from these television preachers, one pastor talked about the time she was memorising the book of Romans. I then thought maybe Romans was one of the easiest books in the Bible, — after all, someone had memorised it. For that reason, I also began to read the book of Romans with the hope of committing it to memory; I failed to memorise even the first five lines. I gave up the idea of memorising a book very quickly.

For a period of four to five years, I thought I was looking for God, yet it was God looking for me. Scriptures tell us that no one can go to Jesus unless God enables them to do so (John 6:65)).

Chapter 5; A Surprise call

Hymn: A Charge to Keep I Have

Having failed to find God in church, I resorted to looking for him in his word. I bought myself a bible and began reading the book of Genesis. I only managed to go through the first chapter, which I did not understand. I then jumped to Revelations, the book was worse than Genesis, I could not go beyond the first five lines. I went back to the Old Testament and started reading proverbs and Ecclesiastes it was in these books that I got a breakthrough. At last, I managed to get something for my efforts.

There is a lot of practical wisdom for every day leaving in these books be it for a Christian or a non-Christian. These books can be read without commentary and still learn something which cannot be said of other books of the bible. When I finished the wisdom books, I continued with Isaiah, in the opening statements of the book, I did not know if it was God or Isaiah talking. After trying many times, I gave up; bible study hour became napping time.

I was sleeping in my bible one hot afternoon when I received two guests. They were my first cousin Harriet with one of her relatives called Ruth (R.I.P). I welcomed them into the house and gave them a refreshment. We talked about all sorts of things including the church situation in Uganda. On hearing my experience with the church, Ruth was of the view that I was mature enough to join a bible study fellowship. She invited me for the introduction class, which was to take place on the first Wednesday of the following month. I had never heard anything about that bible study fellowship but I was willing to try it.

The following month found me ready to join a bible study group. I went to Kampala Baptist church where I found many cars parked in the compound and many women moving around. At the door, I found a young woman who greeted me with a smile. When I told her that it was my first time to attend, she pointed me to the front pews. A white slender woman with sharp blue eyes led us in singing a hymn and a short prayer and thereafter dismissed everyone to their discussion groups apart from the people attending the bible study for the first time.

We were a few people who remained behind, around twelve. The white woman introduced herself to us as the teaching leader and introduced to us an African woman as the substitute-teaching leader.

The substitute-teaching leader took us through the basics of bible study fellowship BSF-a non-denominational Bible study and non-profit organisation whose main aim is to teach the Bible and help individuals enter a personal relationship with Jesus Christ. This Bible study was for serious and committed people who were ready to attend every week. When a member missed three times in a row without a valid reason, he or she was be discontinued. The substitute teacher informed us that someone would be telephoning us, and that person would be our discussion leader. The introduction class was proceeded by a lecture and at the end we were given some notes. I looked for Ruth to say hello and found out that she was the assistant class administrator.

When I returned home and started reading the notes, I could not put down the booklet. The details, the imagination of the writer and the way the application questions had been set impressed me. When I began to complete the lesson at the end of the booklet, I found the questions stimulating my thoughts and leading me to look deeper into God's word for life-changing answers. I knew then that this was what I had been looking for. When the telephone call came from my discussion leader, I was ready to attend and share all that I had learnt.

My first discussion leader was a German missionary with hazelnut eyes and always wore her hair in a fringe. As the discussion was ending, she asked me to meet her after the lecture to take me through the first-day class procedures. In the meeting that followed, she told me about how a discussion was conducted using guidelines. If you did not complete your lesson, you do not participate in the discussion. The group did not wait for anyone; they began on time and finished on time, even if there were only two people. Group members have a chance to pray for one another by sharing prayer requests. Praying for one another, was voluntary, if I did not wish to join it was ok. Lastly, the group had fellowship once a month where we shared what we were learning with one another.

I joined BSF in 2006 and my first year went well, with only one incident worth mentioning. I believe this incident changed the course of my life for the next five years. The incident occurred during one of our discussions. Both the teaching leader and the regional area adviser for Uganda, Kenya and Tanzania visited our group. Seeing them, I immediately thought about my school practice days. To make my lessons lively, I would ask my students to be active when my supervisor came to assess my teaching skills. Seeing these two people, I thought they had come to assess my discussion leader; therefore, I made it my business to make the discussion lively by being very active. My discussion leader had not asked us to do any such thing, and she had never talked about those people visiting. It was all in my imagination and I thought I was doing her a service. I misunderstood the intentions of these people. I am sure they were there for a reason, but I did not know what that reason was. However, I think my behaviour led them to notice me, and hopefully in a positive sense.

BSF academic year ended in May and it was time to think about the future without interference. I had graduated with a Bachelor of Education; however, it was difficult to find a job. My first cousin advised me to study nursing to increase my chances of employment; I applied at Mengo Nursing School. I was happy about the admission but had doubts about nursing being the right career for me.

My doubts about nursing centred on who I am as a person. While some people run to a crime or accident scene, I run away for fear of seeing the injured people in pain. It is a part of our customs to wash our dead before burying them. Yet, when my aunt died, I found myself in a conflict with my family for refusing to clean her face; I could not even look at her. When I receive news of a family member or friend being gravely ill, I do not want to visit them. This is not because I do not love them, but because I do not want to see them in pain. When someone is experiencing too much pain, I also feel that pain. Moreover, I am afraid of death.

Despite knowing all that, I did not dare to back out of the nursing course because I did not have a job and someone was willing to sponsor me. Yet I worried that my cousin was going to spend money on a career for me that I was probably not going to practice. When I shared these fears with a trusted friend, she was of the view that I was just afraid of the unknown. She assured me that, when I start practising I will overcome my fear of pain and death.

I had seven months before joining a nursing school, and I decided to use that time to pray. I told God about all my fears and anxieties. As I continued to pray, I also devoted attention to what God was saying in response to my prayers. So when a man who nothing about my life approached me and asked me if I was a nurse, I took this incident as God's answer-that He willed me to go and study nursing. I started preparing my mind for what I thought was going to happen.

I spent days imagining how life was going to be in nursing school. When I read the circular, it was like returning to primary school. The rules included a curfew at the hostel if one was not on the night shift; cutting and no colouring of the nails; and wearing a uniform, including a belt, socks and closed flat shoes. I did not like what I was reading, but, if that was what God wanted, I was ready to do it.

While I was waiting to begin nursing school, I received a call from an unknown number, and the caller's accent was not Ugandan. She introduced herself as the BSF teaching leader and she wanted me to pray about joining BSF leadership. It was true that I was waiting for the BSF year to start, but I had never expected to receive such a call.

I agreed to the request and sincerely prayed to God about joining BSF leadership, yet I did not hear anything. There was no dream or audible voice. There was no message from a preacher or a Bible verse-there was nothing. I called my teaching leader and informed her that I had prayed and did not hear a thing, to which she laughed. She suggested that we meet at Kampala Baptist Church and talk about it.

During the meeting, she gave me a small interview and talked to me about BSF leadership. I told her that the problem was not only that I had not heard God's call, but also that I was going away in three months to join the nursing school. In response, she encouraged me to be a leader for the period I was available. When the time came for me to leave, I would be free to move on. I accepted her offer, thinking that this was a temporary assignment before I joined the nursing school. In contrast, God had other plans for my life. What I thought of as a service of three months turned out to be service of five years, in which there was no new direction for my life.

God's call came at a time when I least expected it. I was young and had no experience in spiritual matters and insufficient knowledge of the Bible. I was not looking for anything in that direction-I was looking for a career in areas that I had studied and not serving God. Although the BSF leadership did not demand much in terms of resources and time, I took it seriously. For the five years that I served as a discussion leader, I never missed any leaders meeting or class day.

Chapter 6; A Turning point

Hymn; How Firm a foundation

Daily Bible study with the guidance of BSF questions and notes brought about a turning point in my life. I fell in love with God's word, which ended the restlessness in my heart. I had looked for God (actually, God had looked for me) and, at last, I had found Him in His word. The more I studied God's word, the more I realised that all that I knew about God, salvation, sin and human beings were half-truths and, in other cases, pure lies. Most importantly, God answered all the questions I had harboured in my heart.

God and His attributes

The first half-truth that I discovered concerned God and His attributes. I had heard and later fell in love with a God who is merciful (Exodus 34:6-7, 2 Samuel 22:26), kind (Titus 3:4-6, Nehemiah 9.17), all-forgiving (Isaiah 44:22, 1 John 1:9), a good shepherd (psalms 23, john 10:14), the provider of all our needs (Genesis 22:8) and a healer of all our diseases. (Genesis 20:17, Exodus 15:26). I had heard that God is the alpha and the omega, the first and the last, the beginning and the end

(Revelations 22:13), a redeemer (Job 19:25), a rock (Psalms 18:31) and the almighty (Revelation 4:8).

However, when I began to read the bible, I found out that God is all those things and even more. Moreover, those attributes of God, which are rarely discussed in church, have negative implications for mankind.

Holiness is one of those characters of God, which has a negative implication on the side of man. God being holy means that He does not sin nor does He tolerate sin. Since humankind is evil, we cannot approach a Holy God in any way we want (Exodus 3:5-6, Leviticus 11:44-45). God's Holiness moves hand in hand with His anger. In other words, when we fail to honour God as Holy, we provoke Him to anger.

Some of the people who faced God's anger and ultimately faced death because of failing to honour God as Holy include Aaron's two sons Nadab and Abihu who offered unholy fire to God, which led to their early deaths (Leviticus 10). Moses obeyed God in all things except when he struck the rock twice instead of speaking to it to give the Israelites drinking water. God charged Moses and Aaron of failure to trust Him and failure to honour Him as holy in front of Israel. Due to those failures, Moses and Aaron did not enter the Promised Land; they died on the way (Exodus 20:1-13). At the same time, God's anger burned against Uzza when he reached out his hand to safeguard the Ark of the Covenant. Because of that irreverent act, God struck Uzzah to death (2 Samuel 6:6-7).

The positive side about God's Holiness comes from the fact that He sets apart people for Himself and declares them as holy (Leviticus 20:26). In addition, with the coming of Jesus Christ, Holiness is rewarded to all those who believe in him and repent their sins because God has put all our iniquity on him (Isaiah 53:6, Romans 10:9). For this reason, believers can now approach boldly the throne of God trusting in Jesus' finished work (Hebrews 10:19-22, Ephesians 2:13).

Besides holiness, God punishes sin (Exodus 20:4-5, 346-7, John 9:2). The general punishment for sin is death (Romans 6:23) since we are all sinners (Romans3:23); we have to test death (Romans 5:5) unless Jesus returns now. Sometimes God ignores our prayers because we fail to repent (psalm 66:18, Isaiah 59:2). If we persist in sin, the consequence is sinning even more (1 Corinthians 2:14). The result of sin is judgement.

He is a just judge (john 5:30); God has set aside a day in the future when he will judge humanity according to our relationship with Jesus Christ (Revelation 20:13). After that Great judgement, he will reward the righteous with eternal life (Matthew 25:46), while the guilty will be thrown in hell where there is weeping and gnashing of teeth (Matthew 8:12, 2 Thessalonians 1:9),

From those attributes, I understood that the God of the bible is both Great and terrible we should therefore not trifle with Him.

Knowing those two sides of God raised some challenges. How was I to tell people about the other side of God? We live in a world where the majority of the people are hurting, and believe that God is there to make their lives easier. In this harsh world, it is easy to preach and accept a loving God than an angry God who punishes sin. It is therefore understandable why the negative attributes of God are ignored in most churches.

God answered my worries through Matthew 5:13, in this narrative, Jesus tells His disciples to be the salt of the world. To understand the point of being salt in the world, we have to understand the use of salt in everyday life. Salt gives flavour to insipid food, it is a preservative, it heals wounds, and that is what a Christian ought to be in the world. We should give flavour to the people around us, preserve God's word and heal the hurting

Being a preservative means delivering God's word the way it is without covering up or sweetening up things. We are to tell people that indeed God is kind and forgives our sins, but we still leave with the consequences of sin. Alternatively, to say that prayer is communication with God but it is not a tool for demanding what we think we want. That way people will know God for who He is and revere Him (Deuteronomy 6.12, 17.13, 10.20) rather than thinking of Him as a nice uncle who is there to please them.

On the other hand, salt hurts when administered in an open wound, and that is how healing comes about. If we are to take that route, we are going to hurt and offend people. We are offended when our sins are brought into the light; yet, this will lead to repentance and eventually to healing. It is therefore okay to discuss the side of God that most of us do not want to hear about if healing is to occur in the church.

God's sovereignty

Sovereignty is another attribute of God, which I thought I had well understood. I knew that God controls nature (psalms 104.3, Mark 4.39), He controls all rulers in the world be it good or bad, God controls all circumstances (1 Samuel 16.1, psalms 75.7) and He controls Satan (Job 1.12, Revelations 9.2, 20.7).

What I did not know was that God controls all hearts in the universe to accomplish His purposes. He knows each individual's thoughts, motives and plans (Jeremiah 20.2, Mark 2.8). This is evidenced when God harden pharaoh's heart to display His mighty among His people. (Exodus 10:20, 27, 14:4). God moved the heart of Cyrus to help Israel (Ezra 1.1, 5); God places things on our hearts (Nehemiah 7.5).

I was bothered to learn that I am an open book to God. I was ashamed to know that God sees all my pride, my evil thoughts, my sins and perverseness. This revelation made it uncomfortable for me to go to God in prayer. It took me time to be convinced that God's sovereignty over my heart is a good thing. This sovereignty is now a source of comfort and encouragement to pray to God who knows all things.

It was a big blow to my pride to learn that salvation was all a work of God within His nature of sovereignty. Salvation in Christianity means deliverance from evil and its results and consequences. When I first accepted Jesus, it was not because I had realised that I am a sinner. I had accepted Christ for the sake of going to heaven. I thought I loved God enough to reach out to Him.

On reading the bible I understood that we have all sinned and fallen short of God's glory, (Romans 3:23-26), there is no one righteous, not even one (Romans 3:10), we are spiritually dead. Since we are dead in our transgressions, we are hostile to God (Romans 8:7). We cannot on our own go to God. It is God's sovereign mercy, which works miraculously to make us alive with Christ (Romans 5:6-8).

After God works in our hearts, He then offers us salvation by faith in Jesus Christ and not works (Romans 3:22). It is by grace that we have been saved through faith and that is not from within ourselves, it is a gift of God-not by works so that no one can boast (Ephesians 2:8-9). The result of salvation in Christ is for God to justify us. After justification, we now have peace with God through Jesus Christ (Romans 5:1).

The hardest thing to understand is the fact that the people who have not accepted salvation cannot blame it on God. This is so because God as the sovereign being foreknew who will believe and who will not believe, He only works in the hearts of those whom He has foreknown that they will accept Him. Moreover, we cannot talk back to God, the clay cannot question the potter (Romans 9:20-21).

Given that God is sovereign, it follows that He controls all our circumstances be it good or bad. Because of God's sovereignty, murmuring, complaining, grumbling and wailing are sins against God (Exodus 11:4-22, 16:1-16). Even a small complaint about food is a direct complaint against God because He provides us with our daily food (Matthew 6:6, Luke 11:3). To complain is like telling God that we deserve better than what He is giving us or that we know better about what is good for us. God's sovereignty over our circumstances calls us to humbly accept where we are.

My mind was put to rest with the knowledge that I will never go out of God's will even if I sin or do a mistake. This is possible because God's sovereignty means that His plans for our lives cannot be thwarted (Isaiah 14:27, psalm 40:5). Everything that happens

God foreknew it and it is part of His bigger plan for my life.

The commandments

Having studied the Ten Commandments as a child, I thought I knew all of them by heart. While this is true, when I was in BSF. I realised that the commandments carried more meaning than what I had thought.

The first commandment forbids a man from worshipping any other god apart from the one true God (exodus 20:3). The word worship to me meant bowing before statues and consulting small gods. After reading the BSF notes, I understood that to worship is to give a person or an object first place in our affections, which must belong to God alone. To worship God means to put Him first in our thoughts, first in our relationships, first in our work, first in our leisure time and recreation.

We fail to worship God when we look for solutions to our problems elsewhere rather than Him. When we look for meaning in life outside of Him, when our minds are full of selves, our children, our husbands, money and anything in the world. God should be everything in our lives.

The second commandment forbids us from making ourselves idols in form of anything in heaven above or on the earth beneath or in the waters below (Exodus 20:4-6). Until BSF, I had not noticed the difference between the first and the second commandment nor did I notice that the second commandment is the only commandment, which carries a penalty with it.

Now I have understood that the first commandments concern the object of worship while the second is concerned with the manner of our worship. This commandment forbids the worship of the one true God in an unworthy manner or by the use of images. We are to take the utmost care to worship God rightly by reading scripture. Even the thoughts we have about God, which are not in scripture amounts to creating ourselves gods.

The sixth commandment forbids murder (Exodus 20:13). I did not know that there is a difference between murder and killing. To murder is to take away life unlawfully with premeditated malice while killing is to deprive life for a reason. For this reason, any death that is not caused by natural means can be termed as a murder or as a kill. Knowing the difference between the two words, helped to understand the reasons behind the civil law, which permits to kill.

I thought that God had forbidden us to murder for the good of the human race, that we should not destroy ourselves, and for the sake of having a clear conscience. I now understand that God forbids murder because humans have been made in His image (Genesis 9:6). In addition, God is the only one who gives the breath of life (Genesis 2.7); therefore, God is the only one who has the right to take away life.

The ninth commandment states that we are not to give false testimony (Exodus 20.16). I thought that this commandment is limited to the courts of law. I now understand that the commandments forbid lying of any form.

God wants us to be people of integrity, He wants our yes to be yes and no to be no without additional words (Matthew 5:33-37).

I have come to understand the importance God puts on words; I now try to use words carefully. I have moved away from over-talking, making silly jokes that hurt people, taking un-necessary oaths, making promises that I know I will not fulfil, giving my opinion on everything and exaggerating situations. For it is written, that on the last day, we are going to account for every idle word that comes out of our mouths (Matthew 12:36).

What is blasphemy?

I had read in the gospel of Matthew that all sins are forgiven apart from the sin of blasphemy (Matthew 12:13). Given that blasphemy is any sin against the Holy Spirit, I thought that to blaspheme is to abuse the Holy Spirit. However, after a critical Bible study, I understood that to blaspheme is to reject the convictions of the Holy Spirit. The main work of the Holy Spirit is to point us to Jesus Christ; therefore, it follows that blasphemy is rejecting Jesus Christ as Lord and saviour. Since there is one way to God, it makes sense to view blasphemy as rejecting the Holy Spirit's passage to Jesus Christ.

Do all roads lead to God?

At one time, I believed that all religions led to God. Whether one decided to follow Mohammad, Buddha or Jesus, I sincerely believed that they would all reach God. I even supported my friends who changed religion for the sake of marriage; after all, we were all following the same God, but giving Him different names.

This wrong belief was corrected during the study of the Gospel of John. In John 14, Jesus tells His disciples that He is the way, the truth and life and that no one goes to the Father except through Him. I then understood that Jesus is the only way to the father, not one of the many ways. This means that to reach heaven or God, there is only one way and that is through Jesus Christ. All other ways lead to hell.

I then reasoned that, if Jesus is the only way to the father, why do my non-Christian friends have their prayers answered. If Jesus is the only way to God, then their prayers do not reach God. Again, God answered me through the BSF notes, which stated that He is a kind, God. He answers all prayers in whatever form they are offered, yet He only offers eternal life to His children. His children are those who have accepted Jesus Christ as Lord and saviour.

Up to that point, I had associated eternal life with death. I thought we entered into eternal life when we die, perhaps because of the statement 'May her soul rest in eternal peace', which is usually said during vigils, funerals and burials. It was from John (17.3) that I learnt that eternal life begins here on earth into eternality. Jesus described eternal life as knowing God the only true God and Jesus Christ whom He sent.

Working for God

From an early age, I was encouraged to say 'yes' to God in case He calls me. As I grew older, I developed deep desires of serving the Lord; I thought it was the easiest thing to do. As my Bible knowledge increased, I discovered that working for God came at a cost. It involved surrendering to God's will, which means giving up personal ideas. Personal rights and perceived needs. I had big dreams about how my life should be, and I did not want to give them up. Yet Jesus taught that, if anyone wants to follow Him, that person would have to lose his or her life (Luke 9.23). I understood that working for God is not so easy after all.

Miracles or faith?

For a long time, I longed to experience God's miracle-working power. I envied people who had experienced healing through the power of God, so I prayed, fasted, repented and did every good work of which I had heard so I could experience the miracles. I also prayed to God to anoint me with power, so that I could use it to bring people to Him. When I did not experience this power, I began to question how other people prayed. I wondered what unique qualities the people who experienced miracles had that I lacked. With time, I gave up and realised that performing or experiencing miracles was not for me.

God cautioned me about my desires while studying the book of Romans. The answer to my obsessions with experiencing and performing came from Romans (10:6-10), which says that we should not say in our heart, ''Who will ascend into heaven?' '(That is to bring Christ down)' or 'who will descend into the deep?' '(That is to bring Christ up from the dead)'.

The good notes from BSF explained that it requires a miracle worker to go up to heaven to bring Christ down or to raise Him from the dead. Thus, it is wrong for Christians to believe that they can work hard to experience miracles. Paul assured Christ's followers that, to be righteous in the eyes of God, one needs to do just one thing, and that is to believe that Jesus is the lord (Romans 10:8-9).

My teaching leader emphasised the principle that a righteousness of God is based on faith in His word, not on experiences. She encouraged us to act on God's word instead of waiting to have supernatural experiences. Moreover, such supernatural experiences do not necessarily mean that the person receiving those encounters is righteous.

About asking for the anointing to perform miracles so that many people may come to believe in Christ, the good notes from BSF opened my eyes to the reality that miracles have never increased faith in God. For there is no generation that experienced miracles like that of Moses and Jesus, but still, people did not believe .and these are people who moved on foot wherever they went, they relied on natural healing, if those ancient people failed to believe, how about a generation which has been digitised. In conclusion, God's word is enough to bring faith in people.

An understanding character

I have always disliked my mother's character and never wanted to be like her. She irritates me because she is never sure of what she wants, agrees with everyone's ideas apart from mine, never says what she thinks, she is unwilling to stand up for her rights, she is always willing to be led by whoever is available, and lacks firmness. Due to those weaknesses, people take her for granted.

While studying the Bible, I encountered such a person, by the name of Isaac. Isaac agreed to all the plans his parents had for him, whether this involved sacrificing him (Genesis 22-23) or marrying a woman he had never seen before (Genesis 24:1-25, 18). He willingly gave up all the wells his servants dug to avoid conflict with the local people (Genesis 26:16-20). The only time Isaac put up a fight to do what he wanted concerned the patriotic blessing (Genesis 27). This again reminded me of my mum, she gives in to everyone, but the day she is determined to have something, she will do anything to have her way.

The BSF notes led me to understand that God calls such people humble. The Bible contains promises for these humble people, such as God guiding them in what is right while teaching them His ways (Psalms 25.6). These meek people will inherit the land and live in peace (psalms 37:11), God crowns the humble with salvation (Psalms 149.4), and blessed are the meek for they will inherit the earth (Matthew 5.5). Meanwhile,

Peter described a beautiful woman as one who is gentle, has a quiet spirit and is submissive to her husband (1 Peter 3:4-5). What I thought was their weakness turned out to be their strength, and what I thought was my strength turned out to be my weakness.

We were encouraged to pray to God to give us a meek spirit, but I could not pray for such a thing. I could not see myself giving in to people's ideas without offering my opinions. However, what I could not pray for, God used circumstances to force it on me.

Who is a prophet?

In my lifetime, I have met people who call themselves prophets. Such people claim to see and foretell the future correctly. That is how I began to associate the word prophet/prophecy with foretelling. After reading the bible, I understood that a prophet is someone who speaks on behalf of God. Old Testament prophets like Moses, Isaiah and Jeremiah might have foretold the future, but their main work was to speak the word of God.

To understand the word 'prophet' better, we should look at Moses, who did not want to appear before pharaoh because he was not eloquent in speech. God commanded Moses to go with his brother Aaron to speak for him as his mouth. In Exodus (7:1), God told Moses that He has made him God to the pharaoh and his brother Aaron his prophet. Thus, a prophet is a person who speaks on behalf of God and not just a foreteller

Chapter 7; Pain and God's silence

Hymn; Search Me, O God

In my youthful years, my hardships came in the form of dissolved dreams. When I finished school, I had big dreams. I planned to find employment immediately and work hard to reach the peak of my career and be the best I could be. I dreamt of driving a nice car, building my own home, travelling to see the world, and later settling down and raising children. None of those dreams came to reality, and, as I watched the years go by with me accomplishing nothing, I started viewing myself as a failure in life. I inflicted pain on myself by comparing my lack of progress to the people with whom I had attended school, especially those who seemed to be achieving everything I desired. I woke up every day with 24 hours to myself, and I did not know what to do with that time.

Everyday activities became a boring routine. The word suicide more than once crossed my mind. I thought of all the money that was spent on me to attain a good education, and I worried about disappointing my mom by not becoming the person she thought I would be. It was a good thing that BSF had prepared me for the hardships of the Christian life. I had looked forward to experiencing these hardships and to show God how committed I was to please Him. However, I had not counted on these hardships arising in the form of the things that meant so much to me.

My thoughts about pleasing God through hardships were wrong because, when these challenging times arose, I reacted with impatience, with a negative attitude towards God and other people, with self-pity, with passive defeatism, with sadness and bitterness. Despite having good Bible knowledge, I ignored this knowledge and instead reacted according to how I felt. In spiritual terms, I rebelled against God's sovereignty.

My first response to my faded dreams was to pray to God, asking Him for what I wanted. When that prayer did not yield my desires, I thought that maybe I was not using the right words. I, therefore, opened my Bible and used the prayers of our ancestors in faith as models for my prayer life. I asked God to save me from pain (Genesis 34:11) and I asked Him why He had brought trouble upon me. Was that the reason He called me? (Exodus 5:22) I pleaded with Him to teach me His ways so that I could know Him (Exodus 33:31). I asked

Him to show me His glory (Exodus 33:18). I called on the name of Jesus, son of David, to have mercy on me, like the two blind men (Matthew 20:29). I asked God to give me what I wanted (Mathew 7:7).

After offering all these prayers with great faith and high expectations of God's answers, it was a serious blow to my inner self when God decided not to address my wishes. I wondered why God was not answering my prayers, yet I had been honest with Him. A thought came to me that maybe God was visiting me for the sins of my ancestors (John 9:1).

I started on a final prayer about the issue that I thought was hindering God's answers to my problems, and that was the prayer of repentance. I began by repenting all my known sins and then moved on to repent for the sins of my ancestors. God was completely silent and nothing changed in my circumstances. There was no career to speak of, no money to buy myself a car or build a house and no serious relationship. I begged, pleaded, quarrelled, complained, wailed and told everyone who cared to listen to how God had failed me at a time when I most needed Him. In the end, I failed to pray, the burden on my heart was too heavy to put into words. I did not know where to begin and where to end. I sat in silence as tears flowed from my eyes. I felt defeated by my circumstances.

The other thought in my mind was that I was unsure about God's will for my life. I decided to seek God's guidance, with the hope of finding where God wanted me to be, and in that way find meaning in my life. The problem was that I did not know how to hear from God. I invested in Christian books-especially those that talked about God's voice or guidance. These books gave me many practical examples of how God guides His people. One man wrote about how he felt that God was telling him to move from his home state to another state. As he was still thinking about it, everywhere he went, he found cars with the number plates of the state to which he felt God was leading him. He was convinced that this was what God wanted him to do. He moved to the other state and God blessed him tremendously. Another woman wrote about how God speaks through nature. After reading that book, I looked all over our small green compound and wondered what God was telling me through it.

I visited the children's section at BSF and saw how the children were made to lie down after hearing a Bible story. This was to enable them to think about what they had heard about God and prepare them to listen to God in the future. I tried that method as well. After my Bible study, I would lie down in the hope that I would be able to listen to God. Instead, I just fell asleep. On other occasions, my mind would wander to many different topics. I did not know which thoughts were my desires, which thoughts were of the Holy Spirit and which thoughts were of the world or devil.

Until that trying period, I held false beliefs about my character. I thought I was a patient person who loved and trusted God; however, how I responded to my circumstances proved to me that I was not any of those things. Patience is the willingness to tolerate delay. As years passed without getting what I wanted, I expressed my impatience through my attitude towards God. I became angry with Him and started believing that He is not as good as the Bible says. If He were good, He would feel my pain and end my suffering.

I transferred my hope to my relatives, but that too failed. An aunt who lived abroad came to visit us. After assessing the Ugandan situation and my circumstances, she decided to help me move abroad, as she had done. I loved the idea-it meant I would fly away and leave all my problems in Uganda. How excited I was! I envisioned myself overseas and made plans about how I would live my new life in a new world. The plan was for me to apply to a university in the country in which my aunt lived, and then she and another relative would pay some money to the university to ease the visa application process. At the beginning of the following year, my aunt called to let me know that she had placed money aside for my study and that I should apply to the university near her home. This meant I would enjoy free accommodation at her place.

I applied to the university and was offered a place. All that remained was for the first instalment of the tuition to be deposited in the university account. The first relative was ready with her portion of the money, but the other relative gave me the bad news, she had failed to obtain the money. I received this news after a full year of waiting, with great anticipation. It was beyond disappointment-the pain of yet another shattered dream. I wondered why God was doing this to me again. Luckily, my good relative had another plan in mind. She suggested that I wait for another year, in which time she would save more money and be able to pay for the first installation of the tuition on her own, without relying on another person. The excitement and

108

anticipation started all over again. I started praying earnestly that things would work out well this time.

That year was long, but, eventually, my aunt called to let me know that she had all the money we needed to apply for the visa. She had worked out all the arrangements, including finding me a job to start work right away, as I studied. I returned to my former schools to verify my academic papers for the student visa application. The application was progressing smoothly, and then an obstacle appeared. In previous years, the Embassy only required a bank statement from any relative. However, for the year in which I was to apply, the Embassy had changed the rules and now needed the bank statement to be in the name of the person who intended to travel, with enough money for tuition and accommodation. The money should have been in the bank account for at least 30 days before the time of the visa application.

I did not have money in my account; however, I was not going to give up without a fight. I started looking for money to deposit in my account. I only needed to borrow the money for the visa application, and then later would return it to the owners. I moved from office to office of both friends and foes in search for money, made telephone calls and persuaded people. After two weeks, I had only one thousand dollars in my account, and I needed at least twenty thousand dollars. I pleaded with a friend to liquidate her fixed-deposit account, which had eight hundred dollars in it. I mortgaged my mother's land for five thousand dollars and my brother gave me another six hundred dollars. I tried to borrow from a security guard who earned three hundred dollars a month and failed. At the end of all that hard work, I had around seven thousand four hundred dollars only. I needed to raise the balance of twelve thousand six hundred dollars. What was I going to do?

This time, I decided that I had waited for God long enough, and it was time to take matters into my own hands. I was not going to sit around as other people's lives developed, while mine remained stagnant. After much pondering, I decided to fabricate a bank statement. I applied for the visa using a fake bank statement and prayed that the Embassy would not find out. Unfortunately, the visa application was rejected because my bank statement was not genuine. My sin carried a penalty of 10 years during which I could not apply for a visa to that country.

This time, saying that I was disappointed would be an understatement. I was broken. I cried because once again God had denied me what I wanted. I had patiently waited for three years to fly away from my problems. Every day, I had visions of how life would be in another country. I had imagined working hard, making new friends and being happy. Once again, it was a shattered dream.

I started hating God's character of sovereignty. I imagined God knowing all my plans, going ahead of me and blocking my way. I was afraid of telling God about what I wanted because of the fear that He would give me the opposite to hurt me more. I fancied myself lying to God in prayer by asking for the opposite of what I wanted; imagining that He would do the opposite of what I asked, and I would subsequently obtain what I want.

I was a serious Bible student, yet I was engaging in all these behaviours. Although every lesson carried a portion of practical wisdom about my situation, with notes about trusting and believing God, those statements are only easy to hear when things are going well in our lives. How far can you trust God when nothing is going well? When you have no answered prayers in the areas that matter most, when you live in pain and when your circumstances do not change for years?

Scriptures tell us that Abraham waited for years to have a son, as did Isaac. Jacob was a servant for more than two decades, while the Israelites were slaves in Egypt for more than 400 years, and wandered in the desert for 40 years. Hannah, Samuel's mother, waited for years to have a child. In the New Testament, a woman suffered bleeding for 12 years before Jesus healed her in a moment. Bleeding is not a pleasant experience, yet someone lived with it for years.

Why then did I expect things to be easy for me? Was I more special than other people were? No, I am like any other person on earth. We all experience hardships in the form of broken relationships, illness, death, natural disasters and poverty. As God's children, we must entrust these hardships to Him and seek His blessing-something I failed to do.

These negative emotions and circumstances affected my social life. My character changed depending on my emotions. Sometimes I wanted solitude-to be alone with my thoughts. It was during those times that I resented company. At other times, I wanted company and to talk about my problems. I acted as though I had the biggest problems in the world and was suffering more than other people. The only person on my mind were my problems and me.

I became a very complicated person to deal with. I wanted my friends to see things my way and it annoyed me if they did not. I wanted their sympathy, yet, when they gave it, it still angered me. The people who angered me most were those who dismissed my problems as unimportant. I was only lacking a job and having no serious relationship—issues that were not life-threatening. They reminded me of the people who were in hospitals dying of cancer or HIV/aids-difficulties that had no solution. They advised me to forget such small issues and instead live my life.

One Wednesday, while going to Bible study in a friend's car, I experienced one of my mood swings. I was silent for the entire journey and the person seated next to me noticed my mood. She tried to help lift my spirits by telling me that Jesus loves me. It took all my self-control not to shout at her: if He loves me, why was He not responding to my pleas for help?

Despite my mood swings, the people who loved me never gave up on me. My friends were concerned about the trend that my life had taken. I met them occasionally to discuss my situation and receive advice. We all agreed that there was something wrong but disagreed on the way forward. We agreed that my lack of progress in life was because of spiritual causes, which I had earlier tried to correct by repenting for my sins and the sins of my ancestors. (Looking back, there was nothing wrong-I was experiencing delays just like other people around the world.)

Two of my close friends told me that my bondage was because of the type of family I came from. They talked about spiritual mapping, bondages and generation curses. They asked me questions about my dream life. How successful were my siblings and my aunties? I did not see anything wrong with my family, yet they thought that I needed 'deliverance'. They held the view that I should move away from my church to another church-a 'spirit-filled' church. They stated that a Spirit-filled pastor would prophesy over my life and break the bondage. They argued that my church at that time did not have the Holy Spirit, and that was why my life was stagnant.

Their advice meant returning to the churches I had been attending during my search for God. This was no small temptation because the people encouraging me to go in that direction seemed to be doing well. I shared this information with my mum, who had been very patient with me throughout these troubling times. Mom was of the view that maybe I should try to look for that deliverance. Her answer showed me that her faith in me had slowly degenerated. I had a sleepless night, tossing and turning in my bed, with many 'what if's' in my mind. What if they were right and I was wrong? What if I miss God and look back years later with regret? Was there a problem with my church, or was the problem with me? My mind was full of 'what if' this or that.

I thought about the years I spent attending those churches and wondered what I had gained. An inner voice reminded me that, back then, I was not looking for breakthroughs. Now that I had serious needs, things might work out differently. I found it difficult to stop my mind over-thinking. I love sleeping in, but I could not manage this. By 5.00 am, I was already awake and the first rays of the sun found me on the veranda. I think I was suffering from depression.

Despite such difficulties, I still managed to make a decision; I was not going back to the so-called spirit-filled churches. I had walked that path before, and had given it up and changed direction because I had serious doubts about the teachings and miracles there. My struggles in finding a job and status in life were not going to make me turn back. No matter the pain and uncertainty, I had to press forward and believe that one day God would appear.

This was a decision that my mother later supported. She told me that, after thinking about all my struggles, the Holy Spirit had reminded her of Luke 12:31—we are to seek first the Kingdom of God and other things will be added unto us. To this day, I am tempted by the idea of looking for 'deliverance'. This temptation is strongest when God seems to be silent in my life.

My family developed plans to help me achieve something in this world. I acted following their advice, not because I wanted to or enjoyed it, but because I wanted to please them-to show them that I was trying and to stop them hassling me. When their plans failed, they hurt me even more with their words. A family member suggested that to solve my problem of unemployment, I should start a business. She asked me to go around town looking at successful businesses and ask questions about how they ran their business, and then she would give me the capital to start a small business. I tried this approach, but I have never been a businessperson. I do not know how to calculate finances for a business. I do not know how much I should add to an item so that I can attain money for rent, money for transport, money to invest back in the business and money to save. I refused to start the business partly because I did not know how to start, and partly because I was afraid that it would fail and cause me more trouble.

This was not received well by the person who had suggested the idea. She questioned me about what I thought about the future without financial security. She assured me that no man would ever consider marrying me because I had nothing to give to a relationship. Those were hard words to hear, and I was about to hear more such words.

One day, I was walking through town when I ran into an 'old girl' from my secondary school. She had not been my friend at school, as she was two classes ahead of me, but we had a small chat about our lives. I asked her how her children were and she told me that they were growing fine. In turn, she asked me how my children were, and I told her that I did not have any children. She answered that it was my fault that I did not have children because I had aborted them. Her response shocked me. This was a person who knew absolutely nothing about my life, yet she concluded that I did not have children because of my past sins or decisions, which was not true at all.

That statement stayed on my mind until I met other old girls. As usual, we chatted about where the world had taken us until we reached the topic of marriage and babies. Some of these women were married and others were not, but they all had children. Upon learning that I was not yet a mother, they made fun of me by sarcastically asking if I was still waiting for the Lubaga Cathedral bells to ring before I would make a move (Lubaga is the biggest Catholic cathedral in Kampala).

I regret not allowing God to change things for me, I missed seeing God's mighty hand in my difficulties, but I am encouraged to know that, in future, I should let God be.

Chapter 8; Reflecting on pain

Hymn; To God be the Glory

Without pain, I would never have experienced God's control over all things, nor would I have realised how sinful, cruel, insensitive and prideful I was as an individual. The positive aspect that came out of the pain I experienced was a change of character and attitude towards God and fellow Humans.

Before I experienced pain, I thought I was in control of everything that happened in my life. I had been persuaded to believe that I could be anything and go anywhere I wanted. I thought that, with good motivation, determination, the right tools, hard work, education, good manners and negotiation skills, I would have success in life. Now I know that all these things are good to have, but, without God, they are nothing.

Pain made me realise how helpless I am as a human being. Amidst my struggles, the smallest of things was not within my sphere of influence. I could not fly away and leave all my problems behind. No matter what I did, I could not escape the cage in which I was trapped. After pain, I have understood that there is only one person who controls all things, and that is God. He is the silent power behind all that happens on earth. With Him, all things can be. Without Him, nothing can occur.

Having fully understood God's sovereignty and that no one under the sun can stop His plans, I have learnt to surrender to His will. Working hard to change things to be what we want is exhausting and involves fighting God Himself, which is useless because we can never win, and it inflicts a lot of pain on us. If you want peace and joy, surrender to the will of God in your life.

God's sovereignty is not limited to humans and their circumstances alone-it extends to our spiritual enemy, the devil. Whatever the devil brings to us, God has approved (Job 1:6-12). Given that, the devil's power is limited (though that does not mean that we should underestimate him); I have stopped rebuking him and blaming him for all my misfortunes. I concentrate all my efforts on God, who has the power to control all things.

After searching for God's guidance, I have moved away from the belief that God supernaturally guides us. By supernatural, I mean believing that God guides us with an audible voice. I spent hours trying to silence my mind to hear the audible voice of God. I have understood that God is under no obligation of telling us each and everything He is about to do in our lives.

From my experience, I believe that God guides us in two ways; He guides us by His will of command written in His word, and through everyday circumstances. On rare occasions God can guides us through dreams, an audible voice and visions. It is important to note that not every voice you hear nor every dream is from God. Sometimes we want something so much that we dream about it and say ''God told me'' yet it is our own desires seducing us in our dreams.

After mistaking my dreams for God's voice, I have moved away from using assertive statements such as ''God told to this or that'', to cautious using cautious statements like ''I believe God me to do this or that'' thus leaving space for correction in case things turn out wrong.

It is true that we are spiritual beings made of the body, the spirit and the soul, It is also true that some of our problems have a spiritual origin. However, it is not correct to over-spiritualise everything around us. The prevalent teaching that poverty, delayed marriage, death, diseases, dreams and tragedy have a spiritual origin is true. On the other hand, it also true that, much as all tragedies are spiritual, they are also universal. They happen to each individual on fallen planet earth. Therefore, over-spiritualising these everyday problems leave people vulnerable. We start thinking that we are the first people in the world to face such problems and thus we need special attention. This vulnerability makes people desperate to the extent of believing in false gospels in the search for supernatural healing. God in His great mercy has led me to understand that He does all the spiritual healing we need through His Word, the Bible.

Ten years ago, I used prayer as a demanding tool to try to attain what I wanted from God. When God did not give in to my demands, I sinned against Him by complaining and grumbling. Today, I pray and ask God for what I want. Thereafter, I ask Him to do as He wills and not as I want. I tell God that, as He does His will, let Him give me peace, joy and happiness, no matter what He has decided. I no longer judge the effectiveness of my prayers by what God has given me; doing so will mean that God rarely answers prayers. I determine the effectiveness of prayers by the belief that God does what is best for me in a given situation.

Before I experienced pain, I was a self-righteous person. I knew I was a sinner, but not as sinful as people in prison or on death row. I thought I was not capable of murder, hatred, violence or robbery. And that the people who did such things were in a different league and needed more help than I did. Nevertheless, in an attempt to escape from my cage, I lied, I manipulated relationships and I offered mean prayers asking God to punish people who I believed were in my way. Pain brought the entire evil hidden deep in my heart to the surface. I now realise that, without the powerful hand of God, I am capable of every sin. Therefore, I have moved away from being a self-righteous person who thought that she was incapable of murder or robbery, which has changed my attitude towards the sinful world around me. I am no longer surprised by my sins or the sins of other people. As long as individuals are repentant and remorseful about their offences, I am willing to forgive them.

Pain has also made me more sensitive to the needs of others; I cannot dismiss someone's feelings as unimportant. God has made us emotionally, physically and mentally different (Psalms 139:13), and the way we feel and react in a given situation is dependent on these differences. Issues that are important to me might be less important to another person. Not feeling the way another person feels about an issue does not allow me to dismiss their feelings; to them, this issue might mean everything.

I used to employ words carelessly and did not realise the great effect words have on people. Words hurt me deeply, not only negative comments but also unnecessary advice. How I must have hurt others by my words. Today, I know the value of words, and no longer comment on people's physical appearance, unless I am complimenting them. A simple comment such as 'you have gained weight' might leave a friend without confidence throughout the day. Previously, I would make stupid jokes and make fun of people in a negative manner. On one occasion, I called my friend's children 'infidels' because she is a Muslim and her children are not. That comment must have hurt deeply. I now know that I should not make jokes at the expense of other people-it is cruel and very wrong. May God forgive me for the stupid jokes I made, which may have hurt others.

Hurting people is not limited to negative words; sometimes hurt can be caused by un-necessary curiosity. In normal circumstances, curiosity is a good thing; however, digging deep and deeper into someone's life to the extent of prying or interrogating is unkind. It is okay to ask a couple if they are married and if they have children. However, it is not okay to ask why they do not have children. We must remember that things are not automatic, that is to say after a marriage has taken place, it does not mean that children are to follow. There might be many reasons why a couple does not have children. Maybe they do not want them, which is okay; maybe they are waiting for a later time, or maybe they are trying their best to fall pregnant. If the couple is struggling with infertility, you can imagine how tired they are of being asked about children.

It is a positive thing that God has not given me all that I wanted if He had, I would have turned out to be very prideful. I would have thought that those who do not have money in their accounts, those people who rent or live in slams, those people who travel by public means are lazy, they do not work hard to improve their lives, or that is how they want their lives to be. The reality is that God is the giver of both material and non-material things, those who do not have also want, but God has not blessed them. Therefore, the people who have should be thankful and kind to those who do not have.

The sensitive person I have become today does not wait for people to ask me for help; it is not humane to make others feel like beggars. Help came to me in my times of need; hence, it is only right to do for others what God did for me.

I am a fan of social media and I love expressing my political views; however, I am very careful not to post things that might cause young believers to stumble. Posting updates about a new car, posting photographs from a vacation, posting about a promotion or posting about moving into a new personal home is not necessarily negative. However, there might be someone praying for a meal, so posting about vacation might seem as though you are rubbing your success in his or her not so successful life. Your innocent actions might lead them to engage more in self-pity and to question God's goodness.

Besides causing others to stumble, I learnt something about myself while putting my life out there for the world to see. My motives were not pure. I posted about myself to show off, to reassure those who know me that

I was doing fine; sometimes I posted things to cover up my insecurities especially when I was unable to control a situation. Other times I posted to call people's attention and sometimes to get even with others. That is all in the past, the person I have become, thinks hard before posting about my personal life on social media.

Do not be deceived in thinking that there is a life without hardships, whether for a believer or non-believer. We live in a fallen world, which means that we experience pain through death, broken relationships, unfulfilled dreams, poverty, chronic illness, natural disasters and all occurrences in that sector. Nevertheless, we Christians should approach these hardships by placing our trust in God and not in our skills. Some Christian churches offer the impression that becoming a Christian gives you a one-way ticket to a life without pain or hardships. Preachers and pastors in these churches misinterpret scriptures to provide their followers with false hope and wrong impressions.

Jesus can indeed do anything; however, He will not do everything we want because that would defeat God's purposes. I now know that God and His purposes cannot fail. The purpose of God for His children is to conform to the likeness of Jesus Christ. If we are given all that we want, this conformity will not occur. We will instead become spoilt children with neither values nor morals; children who are likely to take their creator for granted and treat Him without respect.

Pain, hardships and failures examined from a prudential light are not negative because they can transform us for the better. As I reflect on my painful experiences, they have made me more compassionate, understanding, kind and forgiving. Having said that, it does not mean that I am always sweet, sometimes we need to be hard to help someone. Therefore, if there is a need, I am going to be hard.

Pain affected the goals of my life. Although I still want to build a career and see the world, I now have a desire to influence people's lives; I would like to give back to the world what God has given me. I would like to help another person understand God the way I have understood Him. Understanding God can only happen by reading the bible as a whole and interpreting it rightly.

Chapter 9; Reflections on the years of service

Hymn; trust and obey

God's provision

BSF operates on the principle that God provides for those He calls. Indeed, God provided for my needs, though not in the manner I had anticipated.

At the beginning of my service, I did not have a bag big enough to carry my folder containing my notes, Bible and prayer book. I carried all my items in a plastic bag (kaveera). Consequently, every time I wanted to remove something from the plastic bag, it would make a loud noise. I felt so embarrassed. I failed to find money to buy a big bag. Later, my friend Cissy (RIP) gave me a large faded black bag, in which I could carry my possessions.

Making weekly contact to my group members placed me under tremendous pressure. I had fifteen group members who I needed to contact by telephone; yet I did not have enough money to contact everyone. I used the little money I had by rushing through my conversations with them. I did not want to be disconnected in the middle of a call, as this would have meant more embarrassment. I had the misconception that the women came to the group because I telephoned them. Later, I understood that their attendance at Bible study had nothing to do with me, but rather stemmed from their love for God. The revelation that everything was about God took all the pressure off me.

My sister looked after me very well, she provided me with clothes, shoes and money. God touched her heart and she did even more than necessary, providing me with mobile phones and makeup. People who knew me by sight thought I had a good job because my appearance implied that I was doing well financially. To this day, my siblings still help me financially whenever the need arises.

I began one BSF year without a single pair of presentable shoes. My sister had given me her old shoes, but my feet are two inches larger than hers are, so I wore them out in a short time. She had already done more than enough for me, so I did not wish to ask her for more shoes. The more I thought about the shoe situation, the more I worried. At the last hour, my aunt came to stay with us for a vacation, and she brought me several pairs of shoes and many cotton dresses. Once again, God was faithful.

I prayed for a car to ease my means of transport, especially during the rainy season. God never answered that prayer and now I can say that He was right, as I did not have the means to maintain a car at that time. He instead brought along a fellow leader and a good friend who gave me a lift in her car every Monday and Wednesday. With a lift, I was never worried about money for transport or about reaching class late and wet during the rainy season.

That was the beginning of understanding God's provision. Supplies came through my family and friends. In most cases, they came at the very last minute and often amounted to exactly what I needed, with little or no extra to spare. The old Susan had thought that, since she was serving God, He was obliged to give her all she wanted promptly.

Lessons learnt in leadership

Leadership in BSF meant serving God and others. As a discussion leader, I had to attend leaders' meeting every Monday to be able to lead my group on

Wednesday. Every Wednesday I had to arrive early to prepare the place where my group was to hold the discussion. I had to organise fellowship for members to share what God was teaching them and for bonding once a month. Although most people look, down at servants, from my experience, the position brings joy and satisfaction.

From the leadership circle, I learnt to pray about things that I thought could easily be fixed without God's intervention. I picked that lesson after hearing fellow leaders pray for a microphone to work and God to protect their time to be able to do their lessons. Before joining the leadership circle in BSF, I would never have thought about praying for such problems. I would just look for solutions. I would take the mic to the mechanics and for time, it would be up to me to reorganise my schedule and find time to do my lesson. Now I know that there is nothing too small for God to help.

At the same time, I understood what it means to be born again. I learnt that for someone to born again, there is a change experienced outwardly, which begins from the inside. For this reason, the testimony of a born again believer should go like this ''I did not know that it is a sin to feel angry and not tell the person with whom I am angry. After reading God's word, I was convicted of what I was doing wrong. From now onwards, I intended to tell people when I am angry with them, with love and compassion''. Believers testimonies should not all be about God gave this or that.

Failures as a leader

Not all went well during my time as a leader. In some areas, I fell short of the required standards.

BSF administrators encouraged us to have quiet time in the morning when we are still fresh. In this, I failed. I could not concentrate on reading my bible in the morning when my house was dirty or when the sink was full of dirty utensils. I imagined a guest visiting that early and finding me in a dirty house. I settled with doing my house chores in the morning and having my quiet time in the afternoon.

Using Matthew 7.7, BSF members are encouraged to pray for one another and to share their answered prayers. BSF standards require a leader to pray for group members by name daily. While making weekly contacts, we were required to ask group members for their prayer requests. The group leader read out the prayer requests to member at the end of the discussion.

I tried to pray for my group members regularly, yet failed. The fewer problems I had in my personal life, the easier it was for me to pray for my group members by name. However, I prayed less whenever I had many problems in my life. I concentrated on myself and only made general prayers for members, such as asking God to provide for their needs, help them complete their lessons and bring them to the discussion on Wednesday. I learnt that a leadership position is not easy; it takes a spiritually mature person to carry both her problems and those of other people. A mature leader can intercede for others, regardless of what is occurring in her personal life, without letting her feelings and emotions dictate how she prays.

I struggled with confidentiality issues. I wanted to share the stories of fellow leaders to my group members. This was because some group members had the misconception that people in the leadership circle had no problems. I therefore thought that if I could give them a glimpse into the lives of their leaders, they could connect, understand and later on be encouraged to realise that there is no perfect human life. Nevertheless, the fellow leaders did not permit me to share their life stories in my discussion group.

Finding other BSF leaders was another role played by the discussion leaders. I failed to make leaders, and I cannot blame this on circumstances. My failure was because of who I was as an individual. Having seen how sweet people could be, and that this sweetness usually presented a false picture of the Christian life, I made it my life purpose not to be sweet to anyone. I aimed to be a matter-of-fact person to those who approached me. Because of this approach, every time I tried to find leaders, I looked for someone like me. I sought someone who was not sweet, was a bit strict and was committed and realistic about the Christian faith. I scrutinised my group members during the weekly contact and monthly fellowship. I used their shared stories as a measuring stick for recommendation to leadership. I did not recommend any person who was sweet and very spiritual.

I can now admit that my method was not the correct way to recommend leaders because we are all different, and hence we experience God differently. Besides, some people will always be sweet, regardless of what they have gone through. The lord God has given us different spiritual gifts. A sweet person may have a spiritual gift of showing mercy to others. Besides, people grow in character and attitudes as they learn more about God and His ways. It was wrong to use myself as a role model for leadership qualifications.

In most cases, it is difficult to know ourselves for who we are. I always viewed myself as having every good character, which is not true. I thought I was kind, gentle and honest until a group member told me otherwise. While we were studying the book of Isaiah, a new class member was added to my group. As a discussion leader, I had to tell her what to expect from the discussion group. With detail, I told her what to expect and how she should behave. After I asked her if there was anything, she had not understood, she replied that I was 'too hard'. The miracle on that day was that I did not get angry with her.

Her comment led me to wonder what I had done wrong. What had I said to offend her? After reflecting on our conversations, I realised that maybe I was very blunt with her. I had warned her that she would be terminated if she missed three times consecutively. I had then asked if she was ready to join the group and, if she was not, to let me know so that someone else take the opportunity. Perhaps this young woman had expected me to provide such information in more gentle words; instead, I offered a 'take it or leave it' attitude. Since then, I have learnt that good leaders strive for a balance-not to be so blunt that you scare people away, and not to be so sweet that you let people take you for granted.

Having realised that being too sweet is not good, I later realised that being too honest is not good either. After one of our monthly fellowships in the leadership circle, a trusted friend took me aside and asked me why I was angry with God. That question meant that, once again, I had negatively displayed my emotions. I did not pretend not to understand what she was talking about; it was very true, I was angry with God for letting me live in such pain, even though I doing what He had set before me with all what I had.

Later, in my quiet time, I reflected on myself as a leader. If a person I was serving with could see my bitterness, what about my group members? What kind of example was I setting as a leader? I prayed and hoped that I was not an obstacle to the young women I was leading. I continued serving for another three years, yet nothing changed in my circumstances. Once the anger and bitterness overpowered the joy and peace that I had experienced through serving God, I knew I had to leave. I did not want people to doubt God's goodness because of my bitter spirit. I decided to retire from BSF and ended up sitting at home, doing nothing.

Chapter 10; Seeing God's hand in every step

Hymn; Guide Me God thy Great Jehovah

After I was denied a visa and for a good reason, I thought it was right to return my aunt's money, which she had deposited in the university. However, she would not hear of it, she wanted me to try again. I had not told her the truth about what happened with the previous visa application. I told her that I had given up the idea of joining the university, as I would not be able to meet the requirements for a student visa.

Given that the university to which I had applied had branches in the Middle East and Asia, we decided that I should try my chances on another continent. I sent an application to the Middle East campus, after which the university sent me an admission letter. I was warned that the master's programs were part-time, which meant that they did not offer student visas. I looked for a residence visa to the Middle East in every tour and travel company and failed to get one. What was available was a stay of no more than three months, yet the master's program would last two years.

I informed the university about my predicament. Luckily, they agreed to send me a student visa via email, with a condition attached to it, I would be subjected to a physical fitness test before they placed the visa in my passport. Until reaching the university visa office, my understanding of a physical fitness test was jumping or running around. In contrast, this fitness test turned out to involve a chest x-ray and HIV test.

I was supposed to start school in September; but because of the visa delays, I instead opted for the February intake. After securing the visa, I asked the university in Europe to transfer my tuition to their branch in the Middle East. I left Uganda for the Middle East on 28 January, with three hundred fifty dollars, which was a donation from my friends. I placed the money in the pocket of my jeans. I had been advised never to put cash in my luggage, but to keep it on my body. Unfortunately, I reached Nairobi to discover that I had lost the money. I think I lost it between Entebbe and Nairobi, probably while using the washroom. That marked the end of my excitement on that journey.

For the five-hour flight from Nairobi to the Middle East, I worried about what was going to happen to me. What if immigration asked for money? What if the man who had promised to collect me at the airport did not arrive? God, why have you done this to me? While I was unhappy and deep in thoughts, my neighbour on the plane tried to have a conversation with me. He told me that he was a businessperson. I told him that this was my first time in the Middle East. When he sensed my reluctance to talk, he stopped trying to chat.

As we disembarked from the plane sometime past midnight, my friendly neighbour invited me to spend a night in his hotel room, with a promise that he would help me find my way the following morning. I gave him a big smile and told him that I had someone waiting for me, although I was unsure if he would be there. Throughout the time we spent in the long immigration line, he kept a close eye on me, until I reached outside.

Before I left home, my mum was worried about me travelling alone to a strange country where I knew no one. She asked some of her friends if they knew someone in the Middle East who would be kind enough to receive me at the airport. My mum's friend Sarah

141

knew someone with whom she had worked with years ago, who had left Uganda for better opportunities. They had not spoken for years, but she asked this friend over the telephone if he could collect me from the airport, which he immediately agreed to do.

I found this God-sent angel waiting for me at the airport. He told me that he had booked me a room in a cheap hotel, which cost fifty dollars for the night. When I told him that I had lost all my money on the way, he sympathised and took me to his apartment, where I slept in the guest room. The following morning, I used his telephone to call my aunt, who agreed to send me five hundred dollars to start my new life in this new country, as I looked for a job.

This person cared for me as if I was his sister; he bought me a telephone and drove me to my university. The administrator at the university acknowledged that a total sum of five thousand seven hundred fourteen dollars had been transferred in my name from their European branch. With the initial money issue settled, we moved on to discuss the course. I had applied for a Master of Psychology, which would cost $13,482 payable in four instalments over the two years. The money paid would cover the first instalment and accommodation, but there were many other problems. I had to pay for a student visa, which cost $2,000.

Additionally, there was one intake for psychology and this happened every September. In February, there was only one-course available-human resources—whose cost was $22,472 payable in four instalments over the two years. As they were telling me all this, my eyes fell on the notice board, where I saw a sign stating that delays in paying tuition fees would be penalised with a $100 fine for each week of delay.

How was I to solve all these problems? The best option for me was to go back home. Yet God was and is still sovereign. The chief account and the dean of students reasoned with me that, because I was already in the country, it was a waste of resources to return to Uganda. They suggested that I should study human resources since it was the only available course in February. When I told them that I did not have the money and that the penalties for delayed payments will strain me they replied that they would be patient and, in my case, the penalties would not apply. When I told them that I did not have the $2,000 for the visa, they suggested that I look for a job to obtain an employment visa, for which the company would pay. Besides, the student visa did not permit a student to work. I left the university with one thing on my mind-to seek a job.

With the money my aunt had sent me, I started looking for work. This was not easy because, although I already had a university degree, I did not have any work experience. Additionally, most employers wanted a resume with a photograph, yet I did not look good. I was overweight with many pimples and scars on my face. I tried to apply for jobs online, but this did not help my low self-esteem. Job advertisements read like this:

- 'To apply for this job, make sure your weight is proportional to your height.'
- 'Come for a walk-in-interview. You must be slim and good-looking.'
- 'I am looking for a maid. The right maid must be Filipino.'
- 'Our company is looking for sales girls, and they should be Filipino only. Africans and other races do not bother.'
- 'Our company is looking for bodyguards and bouncers. We want Africans only.'

- 'To apply for this job, send your resume with a professional photograph.'
- 'Our company is looking for sales executives; they should be Russian, Chinese and Arab speakers.'
- 'I am looking for a well-groomed receptionist with fluent English. Africans, please do not reply to this advert.'

Those online advertisements left me with little hope. To improve my chances of employment, I turned to walk-in interviews. I searched for walk-in interviews online and in The Gulf newspaper. However, the long queues at the walk-in interviews left me overwhelmed-there were hundreds of people. I found some Ugandans with whom I exchanged contact information so we could inform each other about any available walk-in interviews. We all eventually obtained jobs in a coffee company after a walk-in interview at which they accepted all nationalities, except Filipinos and Kenyans.

I started work as a barista in a small mall. From the start, I knew I had made a mistake in signing a two-year contract. My supervisor, Eddy, made it extremely difficult for me to work. He assigned me both café and backroom duties throughout the eight-hour shift. This was okay for a beginner, but the way he did it was cold and cruel. He set a timer to ring every 10 minutes, which meant I had to enter the café to collect plates and mugs and place them in the dishwasher. Thereafter, I would have to mop the café. By the time I finished that, the timer went off again. He refused to allow me anywhere near the till. I had never stood for four hours and my back was killing me, yet Eddy did not let me even lean against the wall. He intended to have me terminated.

After a break of one hour, I returned to do the same thing. Towards the end of the shift, I refused to move, even when the timer went off. Eddy called me, gave me a piece of paper and told me to write what I was doing. I wrote that I was drinking water because that is what he found me doing when the timer had gone off. He was furious and told me to write more. I guess he wanted me to write something that he could use against me. He warned me to be very careful with him. I thanked him for forewarning me about what kind of treatment I was to expect from him. Because of my issues with Eddy, I was late in catching the car that took us to where we lived. The car was already full and, when I tried to squeeze in, a young Filipino girl widened her sitting position, saying that the car was for kabayans only. They wanted to leave me in the parking yard, yet it was past midnight. Finally, a young man from Nepal helped me squeeze in on his seat.

I cried that night with an emotion I could not explain. One Filipino man had done everything in his power to make my life difficult at work, and another Filipino woman wanted the car lift to leave me in the parking yard in the middle of the night. The following day was my off. I did my housework and rested on my bed. In the afternoon, the manager of the café, named Mario, asked me to go to the workplace so we could discuss the report I had written. I did not want to go because it was my day off, and I only had one day off per week. To visit work on my day off seemed like working for a whole week, nonstop. I also did not want to be terminated because that meant the end of my visa, I decided to go.

Mario was a mature man in his fifties. However, it was unfortunate to note that his maturity stopped at his age. He asked me what had happened the night before, and I told him my side of the story. He informed me that I would work with him on the morning shift the next day. I worked with Mario for five days, after which he told me that he was transferring me from his store to another store in a luxurious neighbourhood. I asked Mario why he was transferring me-was it because of the incident with Eddy. He told me that the store at the other location needed a barista.

I knew this was a lie, yet I could not prove it until the last days of my contract. We received a barista, a Cameroonian called Gus, from the airport store. He was bored at my quiet store and talked about missing work at the airport. When I advised him to ask for a transfer back to the airport, Gus told me that due a misunderstanding he had with the airport manager Mario, he had no case of going back. Mario. That statement reminded me of my transfer to my luxurious store.

Working at this new beach store turned out to be an advantage for my studies. The Lord God had overruled circumstances to make them work in my favour. At the new workplace, we worked 12 hours, from 7.30 am to 7.30 pm, including a one-hour break. In exchange for working so many hours, we were awarded two days off, time I needed to attend my master's classes of two full days each month. Later, the master's program was changed to three classes in the evening. I was still able to attend class three evenings per week, though I was always late. On the days that I attended class, I reached home past midnight, yet I had to wake by 5.00 am to prepare for work.

Much as there was a change in my places of work, the management styles did not change. My supervisors and managers behaved in almost the same manner, which I can summarise in one term: workplace bullying. At the beach store, I worked under two supervisors: Jon a Filipino and Jath a sir Lankan.

For some reason, Jon did not want to work with me, and he showed it. He preferred to work with an Indian male barista. A barista's job requires both skills and energy. If a store has a male and female barista, the woman should be at the point of sale and the man to make the drinks. Jon did the reverse—he would assign the male barista to the till, and tell me to make the drinks. I did as I was told without arguing. After a 12-hour shift and a two-hour journey back home, I was always terribly tired. If I reached home and decided to rest a little before showering, I would sleep on top of my bed and in my uniform. I fell asleep as soon as my head hit the pillow. Every morning when the alarm sounded, it seemed I had only slept for an hour. My body size shrank from size 16 to 12.

Eventually, when the male barista left, John's hostility towards me worsened. I then had to do all the hard work and at the same time endured Jon's emotional and racial abuse. I remember some incidents vividly. A customer once walked in dressed in a beautiful pink blouse, and I remarked that it was a nice colour that I would wear any day. Jon replied that I was too dark to be seen in that pink blouse. Another time I was walking with Polly, a very brown Kenyan girl, and was holding her left hand. Jon started walking on her right side and said, 'We are now moving in our colours'. I told my sister about that incident and she told me that I should have told him that we were moving in our heights since Jon was a very short man.

Jon took every opportunity to put me down-he even used my own stories against me. Sometimes life would be very lonely and, in such times, I would greatly miss my mum. On one occasion, I told Jon that my mum used to make fun of my voice whenever I tried to sing, saying that I could not sing. I regretted telling Jon about this because every time I would sing while working; Jon would interrupt, telling me, 'you know, Susan, mothers are always right. You cannot sing at all'. When Jon came to know that I had no children, he would regularly remind me that my biological clock was ticking. Moreover, he called me a 'bitch' and, when the verbal abuse did not drive me away, he tried to convince me that my character was not good enough for customer care. Every morning before I left home, I asked God for extra grace to work with Jon.

With time, I came to know why Jon hated me so much-it was because I refused to steal money for him. While working on the till, Jon would tell me not to punch into the system if the customer was buying a drink, and only punch if he was taking pastries. Sandwiches were easy to follow up than the drinks. I punched everything into the system and Jon became angry towards me. Because of my weak character, I did not report him-something I regret today.

Jath the other supervisor was looking for a promotion. His strategy to getting that promotion was to report to the area manager about each mistake at work. He worked only when the area manager was around, which I found to be embarrassing. How can you be idle the whole day and, when the area manager appears, you start running around? He was cruel and without a conscience.

In my last year at the coffee shop, I worked under a line manager called Ahmed from Egypt. Despite his faults, he was the only line manager I worked with who had a conscience. He never left me to do the work alone; he always helped. He was not a bad person; he just lacked education and emotional intelligence. Ahmed never formed an opinion about the work situation for himself, what Jon told him, it is what he believed to be true. He described my character in the very words Jon used to describe me. At one time, while taking me through an appraisal, Ahmed told me that I had no common sense. Another time, he looked at my passport and came to know my age. That day, he asked most customers who entered the store how old they were. If they were younger than I was, he could tell me, 'Suzanna, this girl is only 15 and she drives a Mercedes' or 'Suzanna, this one is 16 and she's been all over the world'—all those silly comments to show me that I was old and unaccomplished. Emotional intelligence is important in life.

At the beginning of this job, I wanted to give up. I thought about resigning and returning home. However, I thought about the money my aunt had sacrificed to help me attain a better future, I knew I had to stay; I had to endure in order not to disappoint her. I became a shadow of my former self—I was no longer the assertive person who could tell you what I thought, whatever the situation. These circumstances made me a quiet and humble person who did what she was told without talking back. I became very unhappy and miserable because I never did anything right in the eyes of all my supervisors and line managers. On the other hand, not everything about the job was negative.

I was at peace at work whenever it was Jon's day off. I enjoyed talking to our executive clients from all over the world. I loved marketing our promotional drinks and explaining the different services, we offered. Most clients were happy on their holiday and did not mind having a chat. My salary was always paid on time and there was an incremental every year. I started work with a salary of $700, by the time I left the company, and I was earning $ 800.

God, in His sovereignty, saw to it that I was protected at the workplace. He did this by providing an area manager who liked me. Supervisors would give him negative reports about me, but he was always kind. He spoke to me nicely and encouraged me. Jon had asked that I be transferred to another store, an idea I did not like because I needed the two days off and the store was near my university. I needed to stay, despite the challenges. The area manager asked me if I was okay with a transfer, and I said I was not. He ignored Jon's demand for my transfer.

For the two years I spent at the beach store, I struggled with a certain sin-a sin I did not hate but cherished. It was a sin that I nurtured, a sin I was unwilling to relinquish, a sin that I never prayed against, and a sin that I did not repent. I was proud of that sin. Besides my salary, this sin gave me a reason to go to work every day. It was a sin of coveting-I strongly desired something that was not mine. I knew it was wrong, but I deeply wanted it. I was powerless to say no to my sinful desires, yet I knew that if I gave in to my desires, I would be hurt. God in His mercy stood between that sin and me, His power held me back.

The barista job sustained me with my everyday needs and I managed to pay for my tuition. The university stood by their promise not to penalise me for late payment of tuition. Each month, I deposited $400 in their account. My aunt and brother also helped me. Towards the end of my study, I visited the university accounts office to ask about my balance, I was told that I owed the university only $ 50. I paid that money and resigned from my job on the same date that I joined the company two years earlier. At last, I had finished paying off the full amount of $22,472.

There was no financial supernatural miracles-the miracle was God working through people to be kind to me by offering me a job and by allowing an institution to make a special offer to me. God gave me the courage to endure. He also taught me to be disciplined while handling money.

I started to look for other jobs that were not in the field of foods and beverages, as I was tired of that form of work. I hated the mandatory stool test that was taken before the visa for such jobs was processed. I tried other sectors, such as fashion, cosmetics and furniture, yet without luck. In the Middle East when a visa expires, you can stay in the country for a maximum of 30 days without a visa. This is called the grace period. My grace period expired before I obtained another job, and I was scared about a future I did not know. I knew that my chances of finding a job in Uganda were very slim. I had worked hard for two years, yet had nothing to show for it. I prayed to God to give me another job and promised Him all sorts of things if He gave me one.

I stayed at home for two months. Eventually, a friend in the Middle East connected me to the company for which she worked. It was a spa company and I was to work as a cashier/administrator. I signed a two-year contract, and I liked my new job and all the services they offered. I worked in luxurious malls around the country. After one year of working in the busiest centres, I was transferred to the quieter areas of the country. I met many kind Filipinos and enjoyed working with them until I left the company.

I decided to return home to Uganda with plans of linking up with old friends and building solid future relationships. I planned to start a small business and, if the worst happened, I planned to move to another country and start a new life. I placed all these plans before God, through prayer. Yet all those plans failed, and I now find myself in same position I was in ten years ago.

From experience, I have learnt that no amount of fasting, praying or begging can change God's will in our lives. This time, I have decided not to fight God, but to surrender to His will. I have told Him in prayer about what I want and have asked Him to do His will in my life. In return, God has given me peace and joy, despite my failed plans and dreams. This peace is not perfect; it is threatened by deep pain, loneliness and uncertainty about the future. Each time my peace and joy are obstructed by sadness, I return to my Bible notes or my Bible for encouragement. God's word is comforting me. As I waited for the next move, I received an email asking me if I had a story to tell that would help an individual or a family. I hope my story is helping someone so far.

Chapter 11; When a seed matures

Hymn; Lord speak to me, that I may speak

When God places things in our hearts, He sees to it that what He has placed inside us is fulfilled in His way and timing. In my case, God placed the love of His word in my heart. I wanted to study the Bible, yet I did not know how to read it and attain some meaning from it. In answer to that need, God led me to BSF, where I studied His word meaningfully.

Although we did not cover all the books of the Bible, the directors of BSF ensured that we were equipped for personal Bible study. They achieved this by organising seminars in which we were taught how to spend time alone with God (personal quite time), how to study the Bible (homiletics), how to lead others and how to share the gospel. These seminars presented by the substitute-teaching leader and they introduced us to a more in-depth study of the bible on our own.

Group members were encouraged to attend, while each discussion leader needed to attend at least one seminar each year. In the beginning, I only attended to meet the requirements of my calling. With time, however, I learnt to enjoy the seminars. Quiet time, homiletics and the resources for study and teaching became my favourites; I mastered the three seminars well.

When the time came for me to leave BSF and later on live in the Middle East, I put into practice what I had learnt from the seminars. I began to read the Bible on my own without the help of BSF questions and notes. I started with Paul's epistles but moved away from them, they were difficult to understand because of Paul's appeal to intellectualism. I decided to return to the Old Testament, beginning with the book of Joshua. From there, it was easy to connect with people who lived in ancient times. Much as their lives were different from ours in terms of technology and development, yet human problems are the same everywhere. Moreover, the almighty God has not changed-He is the same yesterday, today and forever (Hebrews 13.8).

Through these personal studies, I gained further insight into the ways of the Lord God I have believed. I got these insights from 1 Samuel chapters 5 and 6 in a story of Israel being defeated by the Philistines. After the defeat, the Israelites returned home to mobilise and attack again. In this second attack, the Israelites brought the Ark of the Covenant with them on the battlefield. The ark was a wooden box containing the Ten Commandments. The ark was a symbol of God's physical presence among His people and it had special powers that had given Israel victory in times of war. Upon seeing the ark, the Philistines were terrified, yet they managed to rally themselves to the battlefield.

It seemed to me that the Israelites thought that, by taking God with them to the battlefield, they would surely win. Unfortunately, this was a miscalculation, as Israel suffered a worse defeat than in the first battle. The philistines capturing the Ark of the Covenant and taking it to their territory was the pitch of Israel's defeat. The Israelites must have wondered what had gone wrong. How could they bring to the battlefield their God, who was greatly feared by their enemies, and end up being defeated in such a humiliating manner?

Meanwhile, the Philistines must have thought that having two gods would lead to more success against their enemies on the battlefield. This turned out to be untrue as well because, when they placed the ark besides their god, Dagon, he fell facedown. Their persistence did not improve Dagon's situation-when Dagon was made to stand beside the ark a second time, he fell again, breaking his head and legs.

Nevertheless, the Philistines remained determined to have the ark with them. For that reason, they next sent the ark to other regions in their territory. However, this proved a poor decision because, wherever the ark went, the lord's hand was heavy on the people in those areas. Many people died because of hosting the ark and those who did not die developed tumours.

The ark terrorised the people. As it was transferred into Ekron, the people cried out, 'They have brought the Ark of the God of Israel around to us to kill our people and us' (1 Samuel 5:10). The presence of the Israel God in their territory was causing more harm than good. Eventually, the Philistines decided they were better off with their god, Dagon, rather than the God of Israel. They sent the Ark of the Covenant back to its rightful owners.

The people of Israel rejoiced upon having the ark back; however, these celebrations were short-lived. The lord struck seventy men dead for looking inside the Ark of the Covenant.

It became obvious to me that having God with us does not grant health, wealth and success in all that we do. The Israelis thought that taking the Ark of the Covenant to the battlefield was a sure way to succeed, and they were instead defeated. The Philistines thought that having two gods was a way to increase success, and, instead, their god was broken and sickness overtook the majority of the population.

This ark story gave me insight into one of my daydreams. I have always struggled with hearing God, and I wished to have a one-on-one with Him. I knew that I had God's word at hand and the Holy Spirit to direct me, but I was not content with them. They did not address questions such as what career I should pursue or when was the right time to talk to certain people-problems that could be easily solved if I talked to God physically.

The ark story led me to understand that having God in a physical form is more of a burden than a blessing. A holy God requires holiness, attentiveness and careful obedience from the people who approach Him. Yet as long as humans live in the flesh, they cannot be holy, cannot obey every small command and are subject to fatigue, so they cannot be attentive all the time. I think that the people of Israel must at times have resented the ark. When the 70 people died, the survivors expressed this burden by saying, 'who can stand in the presence of the lord, this Holy God? To whom will the ark go up from here?' (1 Samuel 6:20).

Talking to God physically is not a good idea because I am unlikely to be in a position to meet His requirements, and this failure might lead to my early death. Therefore, I must find contentment in God, the Holy Spirit and the word.

Hymn: I am His and He is mine.